WHAT PEOPLE ARE SAYING ABOUT

THE YEAR OF THE LORD'S FAVOR

Barth once said that the preacher should have the Bible in one hand and to-day's newspaper in the other. Tom Arthur does just that. This is Biblical exposition of a high order, sure-footedly tracing the journeys of God's grace in the lives of his people and the flux of the world. Read these reflections and let Scripture come alive for you.

David Cornick, General Secretary, Churches Together in England

Those who think that nothing of significance is being said in our churches will think again. Tom Arthur counts for me as a great preacher. He boldly addresses the issues of the age with a mind conversant with the most enlightened biblical scholarship. He is both crisp and pertinent. Those who heard Tom preach at City United Reformed Church in Cardiff (thanks to Tom now an 'Open and Affirming' church) were always provoked to think, and challenged to live, in new ways. This book will multiply those so challenged many-fold.

John Henson, Baptist minister, author of *Good as New, Bad Acts of the Apostles* etc.

What makes this book a must read is the way these well crafted reflections bring together experience, contexts and scholarship to open up spaces for readers to make their own connections. Faith is not found in neat and crisp propositions, but in the juicy and sticky stories of our relational encounters. These reflections overflow with freshness, generosity and hope!

Michael Jaggesar, Secretary for Racial Justice and Multicultural Ministries and 2012-2014 Moder[illegible]f the United Reformed Church

Two things are necessary for those who try to expound the scriptures – a deep knowledge, love and understanding of the texts coupled with the ability to see their relevance to our own contemporary life and its issues. These meditations succeed on both counts.
Barry Morgan, Archbishop of Wales, The Church in Wales

A lot of *The Year of the Lord's Favor* is quite hard hitting - and I'm speaking for myself. Tom Arthur brings freshness to familiar scenes. There's not much I read these days that I want to get on to the next page and see what's going to be the next twist, but this is one of the exceptions. And I like the humour. This is my kind of stuff.
Allan Pickard, Union of Welsh Independents minister and BBC journalist.

Tom Arthur's *The Year of the Lord's Favor* stirs my soul and opens my mind to things I had thought I was familiar with, allowing me to see something new. He engages the reader with experiences from his own story and interesting and wide-ranging references to illuminate the scriptures and make them totally relevant to what is happening around us today. These reflections speak to our common human condition; they also expose much of what is wrong with our society – there is challenge, healing and hope here. Through it all the Good News speaks clearly.
Jeff Williams, National Secretary for Christian Aid Wales

Anyone who prepares sermons, or who regularly listens to sermons, knows the hazards and bland irrelevance of sermons that fail to connect. In this splendid book, Tom Arthur eloquently writes about what he calls "the here-and-nowness" of the gospel. Here is thoughtful writing by a pastor/scholar who has served and preached to congregations on two continents and in very different sociological contexts. He draws from his own rich experience and brings to his commentary voices from the world of the arts, literature, politics as well as religion, that is, from the amazing complexity of human life in the world.

This is an important book that will be provocative and helpful to readers, preachers, listeners, and students, alike.
John Buchanan, Editor and publisher of *The Christian Century*

Tom Arthur's well-crafted and passionate reading of Luke's Gospel is a remarkable weaving together of solid exegesis, his own pastoral experience of some thirty years on two continents, and incisive reading of contemporary events in light of Luke's prophetic portrayal of Jesus. Strongly recommended for preachers, those interested in contextual theologies, and anyone caring about a ministry of social justice in today's world.
Robert Schreiter, Catholic Theological Union, Chicago; author of *Constructing Local Theologies*

Good biblical exposition, like good preaching, needs to connect with people as well as connect with the text. It also needs to connect with current issues. These racily written reflections on the lectionary's year of Luke texts do all three as well as at the same time presenting the writer as a real person. Engaging and challenging, entertaining and confronting, they "play it again", as one the titles puts it, faithfully presenting what has been the heart of the gospel from the beginning, but doing it in ways that keep it new and fresh.
William Loader, Murdoch University, Western Australia

The Year of the Lord's Favor

Proclaiming Grace in the Year of Luke

The Year of the Lord's Favor

Proclaiming Grace in the Year of Luke

Tom Arthur

Circle Books

Winchester, UK
Washington, USA

First published by Circle Books, 2012
Circle Books is an imprint of John Hunt Publishing Ltd., Laurel House, Station Approach,
Alresford, Hants, SO24 9JH, UK
office1@jhpbooks.net
www.johnhuntpublishing.com
www.circle-books.com

For distributor details and how to order please visit the 'Ordering' section on our website.

ISBN: 978 1 78099 755 1

A CIP catalogue record for this book is available from the British Library.

Design: Stuart Davies

Printed in the USA by Edwards Brothers Malloy

CONTENTS

Foreword

I am impressed, touched, moved and inspired by what I read in *The Year of the Lord's Favor*. I am impressed by its honesty, its openness, its use of literature and the arts, its sense of reality and its powerful speaking to readers and hearers. Above all, I am impressed by its firm rootedness in the local and global context which shapes these reflections.

For Karl Barth, preaching and theology are bound together. Theology is not an isolated discipline far removed from the life and witness of the Church but is rather shaped by (and, of course, shapes) the Church's constant struggle to articulate the faith in a particular place, among a particular people and for a particular moment in history. Tom Arthur's reflections share this same conviction. They emerge from the Reformed tradition and enable this encounter between God's Word in Scripture and the context of our Christian life and prophetic witness to speak to us in powerful ways and to contribute creatively to a shaping and reshaping of a theology for our day.

But they emerge also from a particular context, or, more accurately, particular contexts: inner-city Chicago in the USA; an urban priority area in Cardiff, South Wales; a leafy Birmingham, England, university community; and a vibrant Cardiff city center church. All these required Tom to enable God's people together to engage with the contexts in which these churches were set, to allow God's Word 'to speak truth to power' and to people alike, and to be faithful disciples and witnesses in the communities in which they were set. These reflections should encourage all of us who are preachers to learn these contextual lessons, for ourselves and for the congregations we serve Sunday by Sunday.

There are at least two approaches to preaching that is guided by Scripture. One is to use Scripture as a means of articulating our own faith, a kind of *eisegesis* that is always in danger of reading into Scripture what we want it to say to us and to our people. The other is constantly and faithfully to allow Scripture to speak to us – often in uncomfortable ways – to challenge our thinking and our action, to bend us in repentance and to open up for us the joys and hopes, the love and compassion of the Gospel's forgiveness, grace and promise in Jesus. Tom Arthur's reflections are deeply rooted in this latter approach. He takes the text seriously and lets it speak to us (and to him) and does not use the text to say what he wants to say. What we receive is radical, not in any frightening or threatening sense, but in the sense that these reflections take us to the roots of the Gospel as Luke has understood it and the same radical, challenging Gospel that we are called to believe and obey as disciples of Jesus in our day and place.

I am struck by the fact that these reflections are published in 2012, 350 years after The Great Ejectment of 1662. In one sense, that event was not so much an 'ejectment' but a radical decision by our nonconformist forebears to leave the Church of England as it was at that time because they felt called to a ministry and a discipleship that they did not feel able to fulfill within that Church. One of the convictions that impelled that decision was their urgent sense of being called to proclaim the Gospel in more scriptural, powerful, articulate and relevant ways to the people of these nations. Whatever other lessons we might learn from the anniversary of 1662, this surely must be one of them: that radical, challenging and liberating Scriptural proclamation is still essential to the Church's witness, however many other means of communication may now be at our disposal. So all preachers should read these reflections and the thoughtful and articulate Introduction that sets out how Tom Arthur understands what he is doing in these texts! I cannot preach them where I am – any more than you can – for our contexts are different. But our preaching today and tomorrow will be greatly enriched through these reflections. We are greatly in Tom Arthur's debt.

Noel A Davies, OBE
School of Theology, Religious Studies and Islamic Studies,
The University of Wales Trinity Saint David
Formerly General Secretary, Cytûn: Churches Together in Wales
Minister, Ebeneser Newydd Congregational Church, Swansea
June 2012

Preface

François Bovon, in his *Hermeneia* commentary on Luke, says: "Luke desires Christians who are concerned with people, not laws, and whose self-identity is that of loyal, cheerful, free, uncalculating, socially aware, devout disciples of the Resurrected One." This describes the Christians I have been privileged to serve as precisely as anything I could write myself. In many ways what I have shared with church people and written about here is what Luke writes about in a Gospel that seems to emerge from his generation's experience to become a pattern for Christian life today.

When I think of the people I have served, whose experiences, questions and insights populate this writing, I think of the Jesuit poet Gerard Manley Hopkins, who loved all things Welsh and even thought of himself as at least half Welsh. He wrote, "Glory be to God for dappled things… / Landscape plotted and pieced – fold, fallow, and plough." I have had the pleasure to serve people here in Wales and in England and in the States whose "pied beauty", to use Hopkins' phrase, is never content with what is flat, prosaic or lacking in passion. They make a perfect medium for exploring Luke in the context of today's decisive moments.

The particular ground from which these explorations have emerged was the course on Luke I taught in the Cardiff Adult Christian Education Centre. Several of the pieces in this collection have their origin in a weekly series of thoughts I had been contributing to the National Synod of Wales' website some years back, a project initiated by Helen Stenson of the synod staff. All have emerged from the experience of pastoral ministry.

It is important for me to give thanks here to members of the churches I have served both in the UK and in the States whose reactions and commitments have done so much to shape my understanding of the Jesus story. I wish I could name them all. I thank Helen Stenson, my wife Marieke and my sharp-eyed friend Ivor Rees, who often came back to me with comments like, "You can't say that!" They encouraged the good Christian labor of critical revision and saved me much embarrassment. And I wish to give a special thanks to friends and colleagues Gethin Abraham-Williams and Kim Fabricius here in Wales and, in the States, Lowell Fewster, whose encouragements and challenges have given much support for this project and for my pilgrimage in general. Life is a community project.

Tom Arthur

Introduction

The Year of The Lord's Favor: Proclaiming Grace in the Year of Luke

In Luke 4, in his hometown Nazareth synagogue, Jesus reads from the scroll of the prophet Isaiah to proclaim the year of the Lord's favor (Luke 4:19). And he says, brazenly, that this scripture has been fulfilled in our hearing. How can this assertion be true? What does it mean to make such a proclamation in a world as complex, as compromised then as it is now?

Proclamation Here and Now

Reading Luke, we can't hide in the future. This text stands in the place where Mark and Matthew had Jesus proclaiming that the kingdom was coming soon. Luke is saying it is here. When we preach from Luke we need to enlist the context of our proclamation, the here-and-nowness of our historical situation, as the medium of the text's interpretation and confirmation. The proclamation of the year of the Lord's favor needs to connect honestly and realistically with the ordinary circumstances of where people are.

The following reflections on the texts of the Revised Common Lectionary's year of Luke are attempts to wrestle with this question. They are written in the conviction that God's Word becomes audible for us only when it is incarnated in human experience, in politics, among lovers, at the workplace, in birth and death. "Wherever there is theological talk," Barth told a group of Leiden students in the politically charged early months of 1939, "it is always or implicitly political talk as well." Conversely, it is also true that political talk is always, at least implicitly, theological talk.

So my writing on these lectionary texts is not scholarly, expository analysis of the texts as texts. What I am offering here is a reading of the texts as they are embedded in the cluttered kaleidoscope of personal, social and political history. This journey through the year of Luke is a pilgrimage through a populated landscape, an exploration of the good news as it is contextualized in and resisted by the ordinary experience of life. Necessarily, therefore, these reflections emerge from my own personal journey, first as a young pastor in Chicago, and then later serving in Wales, as much as they emerge from the texts themselves. Valid interpretation is always contextual in this sense. Interpretation is never universal or perennial, though it can pretend to be.

Corrupted Proclamation

What does it mean to proclaim the year of the Lord's favor in a truly incarnate, contextualized sense? First of all, I think we need to recognize the brokenness, the inconsistencies between biblical proclamation and the truth of the world we live in. I remember as a graduate student in literature at Indiana University reading a book by William May, who at that time was the chair of a new program in theology there. In *A Catalogue of Sins: A Contemporary Examination of Christian Conscience*, he said, "Comfort is cruel if it is based on an illusion; counsel ruinous if it advances falsehood; life only collapses into death if it feeds off a lie." The words seared themselves into my thinking and became a central conviction in the ministry I would take up a decade or so later.

In the America of my youth the idea that our world had been blessed provided the sacred canopy beneath which we lived in confidence. The sense of being an elect nation in a promised land was a myth that owed much to the Calvinism of the original European settlers. Early on, Calvinists found it difficult to deal with the profound, inexorable mystery of predestination, and sought means to soften it with evidence for their own election not only through a sense of inner certainty of salvation but also in putative divine blessings on their external lives.

But such self-assessment required a certain blindness to how blessing can require the suffering of others. The house in which I experienced a very pleasant growing up tells this story. It was church owned, a manse, as my father was a Presbyterian minister. Someone had left a bequest, which enabled the church to buy this property and us to move out of the rather cramped quarters we'd occupied for the first two years of my father's tenure as a minister in this central Indiana town. The story I remember is that the house had come on the market after the previous owners had divorced, and the divorce had something to do with the anti-communist fever that had gripped my home country in the years after the Second World War. The husband, apparently, had been blacklisted, lost his job, and the marriage broke up.

I remember overhearing my parents talking about McCarthyism the way Stephen Dedalus, in James Joyce's *Portrait of the Artist as a Young Man*, recalls the adults of his childhood world speaking about Irish politics, not quite catching what the conversation was all about. What my child's mind did catch of it was that my parents didn't like Joe McCarthy, and my father felt ashamed about the circumstances in which the manse had been acquired. The roomy manse, with its expansive lawns and maple, willow and peach trees, was stained with a story of suffering that was more than the suffering of a particular individual. It was a suffering that belonged to a grim moment in the history of the American people as a whole.

This house, with its history, can be a kind of metaphor for the world in which I came of age. On the surface it looked idyllic, blessed. But just outside our town, on what we called the

National Road, was a billboard with a picture of Dr. Martin Luther King Jr. sitting around a table with several others. The caption read, "Martin Luther King at communist training camp." Only after moving to the UK in the late 1980s did I discover, in a *Guardian* article, that there were roadside billboards like this scattered all across the United States, and that they had been put there by the FBI.

The propaganda we lived with told us we were blessed, but must remain vigilant. The message was all pervasive, not just as the filter of the information we received but also as the shape of things. By the shape of things I mean, for instance, the way the flight to the suburbs, according to urban sociologist Richard Sennett in *The Uses of Disorder*, was a flight to a clean space where the richness of human diversity is less important than the desire to avoid pain by creating an order of living that is free of diversity and so free of conflict. Such spaces carry with them a susceptibility to certain kinds of ideology.

Gibson Winter, in *The Suburban Captivity of the Churches*, tells how the post-war suburban building boom meant "exclusion from the central city and confinement to the iron cage of conformity" where local churches became "the instruments of middle class conformity" rather than a reconciling force in racial, class and ethnic diversity. Churches were packed in those days, but not necessarily with people hungry for the Gospel. This iron cage of conformity so dominated church life that anyone truly devout was forced to seek religious nurture outside the Church, in poetry perhaps, at the movies, or in groups that engaged in social action.

As churches lost the capacity to serve a truly open and mixed public, so public spaces in general, as Richard Sennett shows in *The Fall of Public Man*, began to disappear. A post-war middle class vision of a comfortable, at-home suburban security led to planning neighborhoods that excluded little bars, shops and pool halls which had been public areas of social interaction. These were replaced by the mass culture of the shopping mall, providing the perfect anonymity for societies that no longer wanted to be neighborhoods. Such social constructions lead naturally to what Richard Hofstadter, in his classic essay, "The Paranoid Style in American Politics", describes as a mode of social behavior and political action motivated by "fundamental fears and hatreds, rather than negotiable interests."

The design of 1950s suburban life could be seen in the public rituals, the parades, the little patriotisms of civic pride and the enthusiastic support for school football teams. Hands over our hearts, we stood to recite the pledge of allegiance at the beginning of every school day, and in the early 1950s they added the phrase "One nation *under God*" to the pledge. Even as a seven-year-old I was uncomfortable with that. The chancel of every church displayed an American flag, and you couldn't get rid of it. When television became part of domestic life, the end of the day's programming was accompanied by a scene of fighter jets roaring across the screen while *The Star Spangled Banner* played. But these were simply the overt signs of a shared self-understanding of blessing that constructed the world we lived in, determined what would sell, determined what would draw a crowd, what politicians had to promise. The covert activities of those who self-consciously engaged in propaganda would never have worked without this kind of shared social vision, some would call it paranoia, that animated suburban American life in the Cold War years of my youth. The Martin Luther King billboard that stood just beyond the city limits would not have been there if the people had not somehow felt affirmed by its presence.

God Bless America, we sang, a patriotic song Irving Berlin had composed in 1918 and revived in 1938. People have been thrown out of baseball stadiums for leaving their seats to go to the toilet or for refusing to stand while it is being sung. Like *God Save the*

Queen, which prays for God to "scatter her enemies / and make them fall; / confound their politics, / frustrate their knavish tricks", it celebrates blessing as an us-against-them thing.

The sense of being blessed by right in this sense was something we held in common with Luke's Israel, though the social configuration of his world was vastly different from the world in which I came of age. While America's sense of blessedness has in large part been based not just on the public myth but also reinforced by its economic and military muscle – with less than 5% of the world's population, for instance, the US consumes 25% of the world's fossil fuel resources and, even in hard economic times, with only 9% of its population in manufacturing jobs it produces 21% of what the work consumes – the blessedness of Judah in the time of the Roman occupation was largely a matter of sacred memory and a longing hope animating disaffected Zealots and the literature of the apocalyptic. The biblical proclamation of the year of the Lord's favor was a matter of deep-seated cultural hope.

The Proclamation's Roots: Biblical Blessing

In order to understand the proclamation of the year of the Lord's favor, we first need to recall the place of blessing in biblical tradition. Blessing is central to the biblical message. In the Old Testament God blesses the goodness of creation, and especially humankind (Genesis 1:28; 5:2). "Be fruitful and multiply, and fill the earth." I remember a colleague telling me once that the word of 'rain' and the word for 'grace' in some African language were the same world. Blessing sustains life. The long genealogical lists in Genesis and Chronicles are evidence of such blessing. As Abraham Joshua Heschel once said, "Just to be is a blessing. Just to live is holy." For the most part blessing in the Hebrew Scriptures is as we see it in the Psalms: "Blessed be the Lord." God is blessed because God has blessed us, as in the blessing of Abraham:

> I will make of you a great nation, and I will bless you, and make your name great, so that you will be a blessing. I will bless those who bless you, and the one who curses you I will curse; and in you all the families of the earth shall be blessed.
> – Genesis 12:2–3

Blessing brings with it the responsibility, often forgotten, to be a blessing. If blessing is what God is all about, blessing is what we should be all about. So references to God's blessing of Israel appear in Deuteronomy with the added twist that the blessing is tied to the people's faithfulness, and the choices we make in life are, consequently, choices between blessings and curses. Get the force of the word "if":

> If you heed these ordinances, by diligently observing them, the Lord your God will maintain with you the covenant loyalty that he swore to your ancestors; he will love you, bless you, and multiply you; he will bless the fruit of your womb and the fruit of your ground, your grain and your wine and your oil, the increase of your cattle and the issue of your flock, in the land that he swore to your ancestors to give you.
> – Deuteronomy 7:12–13

A central aspect of Old Testament blessing was the blessing of fertility. We see that theme in the way the opening of Luke's Gospel evokes the stories of Sarah (Gen 17:15–17) and Hannah (1 Sam 1:10–20): "The barren has borne seven, but she who has many children is forlorn," the once-barren Hannah sings in gratitude (1 Sam 2:5). Mary's Magnificat in particular evokes Hannah's song in 1 Sam 2:1–10, and the story of Mary's own pregnancy is built on another instance of the blessing-as-unexpected-pregnancy story in Isaiah 7:14.

But in Luke blessing is accompanied by the deuteronomic

and prophetic theme of doing justice and acting righteously. Remember how a woman in the crowd calls out, "Blessed is the womb that bore you and the breasts that nourished you." Jesus says, in response, "Blessed rather are those who hear the word of God and obey it" (Luke 11:27–28).

Luke's Gospel starts with the blessing of fertility as a metaphor for the Lord's favor, but, in the Magnificat, for instance, which focuses on the redress of injustice, Mary says that "his mercy is for those who fear him" (Luke 1:50). Mary is singing about real social justice, the kind of liberation of oppressed people (whom she personifies) that we see in the Exodus story, for instance. The Magnificat canticle isn't just a nice little piece of liturgy. In the 1980s the right-wing government of Guatemala banned its public recital. The Magnificat both blesses those who suffer and celebrates them for acting justly in their adversity.

The Proclamation's Roots: Jubilee

The next thing we need to recall in order to understand the proclamation of the year of the Lord's favor is the idea of a jubilee year, stemming from Leviticus 25. Readers will be familiar with the idea of jubilee from the Jubilee Debt Campaign, the successor to Jubilee 2000, which had been organized in the 1990s as a way of celebrating the millennium. The Jubilee described in Leviticus was to be a once-every-fifty-years relief of indebtedness, freeing of slaves and restitution of land to its original owners, who may have been forced to sell in adverse economic circumstances. At the end of seven times seven years (49 years):

> You shall have the trumpet sounded loud... on the day of atonement... And you shall hallow the fiftieth year and you shall proclaim liberty throughout the land to all its inhabitants. It shall be a jubilee for you: you shall return,

> every one of you, to your property.
> – Leviticus 25:9–10

Today's public consciousness has been taken over by the global economic collapse that came when the debt bubble burst in 2008. But in the 1990s the Jubilee 2000 campaign was already telling us about the reckless and self-interested loans that the wealthier nations were making to the world's poorest countries. Much of the current unsustainable debt of the poorer countries is still left over from the 1970s. According to the Jubilee Debt Campaign website, the poorest 48 countries in the world have debts totaling US $168 billion, while for the poorest 128 countries it is over US $3.7 trillion. We see in the irresponsible lending to the poorest countries the same exploitation of the poor that we saw in the reckless sub-prime mortgage lending that in large part sparked economic havoc in 2008. But compared with the crisis of the Euro, the continuing debt crisis of the poorer countries is no longer newsworthy.

So what we read in Isaiah 61 (the text Jesus is reading in Luke 4) is a vision of return from exile in words that evoke the jubilee proclaimed by Leviticus:

> The spirit of the Lord God is upon me, because the Lord has anointed me; he has sent me to bring good news to the oppressed, to bind up the brokenhearted, to proclaim liberty to the captives, and release to the prisoners; to proclaim the year of the Lord's favor.
> – Isaiah 61:1–2

Here we find blessings more sharply aligned with justice and with hope of the reversal of fortunes for a disenfranchised people, and less with fertility and rain for the harvest. Quoted in Jesus' inaugural act of ministry, it establishes the framework for the entire Lukan narrative, for its characteristic concern for the poor, for its celebration of grace and the joyful experience of reversed fortunes. And insofar as such an agenda is rejected by the elders of the Nazareth synagogue, it also establishes the framework for the resistance to the ministry of Jesus in general and for his crucifixion. The word for 'favor' in the Isaiah text as it is quoted in Luke 4 is another variant in the family of words for 'grace': "*dektos*." Luke modifies the proverb used by Mark and Matthew to say: "No prophet is accepted [*dektos*] in the prophet's hometown" (Luke 4:24; Mark and Matthew had said, "Prophets are not without honor, except in their hometown," Mark 6:4).

The World Upside Down

Mary celebrates a God who turns the world upside down, who "has brought down the powerful from their thrones, and lifted up the lowly," who has "filled the hungry with good things, and sent the rich away empty" (Luke 1:52–53). Old Simeon sees it: "My eyes have seen your salvation" (Luke 2:30). Think of the continuing instances of "seeing" in Luke, from the shepherds who hurry down to Bethlehem to "see this thing that has taken place" to Zacchaeus, who "climbed a sycamore tree" to see Jesus, to the diners at Emmaus whose "eyes were opened." In Acts Paul will say his mission to the Gentiles is "to open their eyes" (Acts 26:18). The multitude of characters that populate Luke's narrative are both actors and spectators. What they "see" is what the elders of the Nazareth synagogue fail to see: the year of the Lord's favor whose present reality Jesus is proclaiming and living out and calling his people to affirm as the more fundamental reality.

The multitude of voices in Luke and especially in Acts evokes the atmosphere Russian literary critic Mikhail Bakhtin has called "carnivalesque", a joyful, chaotic community that challenges the stiffness of traditional respectability, those who have too much invested in the way things are to think outside the box, to think outside the traditional interpretations of the Hebrew texts, for instance, or to think outside the imperial high culture of the Greco-Roman world. The rigid worlds of traditional authority simply could not comprehend the hope of the disenfranchised for something different. From one perspective such hope was blasphemous. From another it was folly. The disenfranchised, the poor, the stigmatized, the captive, the good-as-dead, those to whom the proclamation of the year of the Lord's favor especially speaks, lived with an awareness of other cultural possibilities and other ways of naming their world, which freed them from the tyranny of their own inherited language, myths and cultures. Such a situation gives us a key to understanding the way the Gospel of Luke and its continuing story in Acts journeys from Galilee to Jerusalem to Antioch to Rome, a conceptual journey of ideas and cultural re-orientations as much as it is a geographical journey.

The Gospel and especially its companion, Acts, can be characterized in large part as a dialogue between what the traditional authorities see (Jewish, Roman) and the perspectives of a kaleidoscopic, marginalized diversity whose eyes have been opened. The cultural crisis comes to a head at the Jerusalem Council, which Luke places at the center of Acts as he had placed the story of the Prodigal – "This brother of yours was dead and has come to life" (Luke 15:32) – at the center of the Gospel.

In Acts the Jesus people are accused of "turning the world upside down" (Acts 17:6). According to Bakhtin, this is what carnivalesque does. Its irreverence for traditional authority creates a comic reversal in which the clowns and misfits come to reign. Here we have a wonderful understanding of Luke's concept of "grace".

Grace, as a joyful reversal of fortune, is central to the Gospel of Luke. "You have found grace with God," Gabriel tells Mary

(Luke 1:30). The "grace of God" is upon Jesus as he grows (Luke 2:40). The motif of grace, favor, goodwill (*charis*) is particularly strong in Luke with its cognates, words like "joy" (*chara*) and "rejoice" (*chairō*). In Luke 1:14 we read: "You will have joy (*chara*) and gladness, and many will rejoice (*charēsoutai*) in his birth." In Luke 10:17 the seventy return "with joy" (*charas*). Luke 15:7 tells us there will be "more joy (*charas*) in heaven over one sinner who repents." The woman says, "Rejoice with me (*sugcharēte moi*), for I have found the coin that was lost" (Luke 15:9), and the father of the Prodigal says, "But we have to celebrate and rejoice (*charēnai*), because this brother of yours was dead and now has come to life; he was lost and has been found" (Luke 15:32). In such joy we find the mystery of the resurrection. Recognizing the central position of the story of the Prodigal, who was dead but has come to life, which occupies the exact mid-point of Luke's Gospel, gives us a key to Luke's governing theme and to the proclamation of the year of the Lord's favor as its inaugural statement.

The Chaplinesque irreverence of the clown and the intensity of the apocalypticist have in common this vision of joy in comic reversal. In Acts 16:26, for instance, we have that incredible scene in which an earthquake loosens the chains of the imprisoned Paul and Silas. This is like the Roadrunner cartoon character Wile E. Coyote being flattened by an immense boulder and popping up again unscathed to resume the chase. You can do this sort of thing in stories and cartoons. It has a certain narrative logic.

Proclamation and Social Change

To proclaim in Hebrew is *qara'*, to call out. The root meaning of the word carries with it the sense of accosting someone. There is an urgency in the meaning of this word. In Greek proclamation is *kērussō*, to call out publicly in the manner of a town crier. When Jesus says, "Today this scripture has been fulfilled in your hearing" (Luke 4:21), he is underlining the public urgency of the proclamation. Though Luke will often stress the readiness required for an anticipated future ("Be dressed for action and have your lamps lit," Luke 12:35), there is always this sense that what is anticipated is already happening and demands acknowledgement and response. Simeon's eyes see the long-awaited moment has arrived. And to the Pharisees Jesus says, "The kingdom of God is among you" (Luke 17:19). There is a kind of indicative tense, an 'is-ness' about this proclamation. It is a disclosure, an urgent invitation to observe what the ordinary pattern of our days has obscured. The proclamation rides on the Greek notion of truth as *alētheia*: what is no longer *lēthē –'forgotten', 'disregarded'*. The proclamation of the year of the Lord's favor makes clear what is happening now.

Secondly, there is also an imperative sense to the proclamation. The word "today" in Luke 4:21 carries with it a deuteronomic urgency:

> I have set before you life and death, blessings and curses. Choose life so that you and your descendants may live.
> – Deuteronomy 30:19

Or, as we have it in the deuteronomic history, "Choose this day whom you will serve" (Joshua 24:15).

The proclamation of the year of the Lord's favor opens our eyes to the imperative of a new Exodus that is, for Luke, no longer a matter of the past but a choice to be made here and now. Will we live under Pharaoh or will we live in freedom? The year of the Lord's favor is good news that we would do well not to 'spiritualize' or turn into news of a merely personal salvation, or put off to an afterlife. When we proclaim the Lord's Jubilee we need to retain the sense that we are being invited to see new possibilities in a particular political, historical context, where good news makes sense to the poor who need to hear it.

The good news of the Jubilee proclamation addresses questions arising from local circumstances, questions of lost identity and worth, hunger for liberation and the community's economic viability. The good news opens the eyes of communities who are denied power and experience violence, and enables them to become conscious of their oppression and of the possibility of salvation, not as an otherworldly rescue but as a transformed world enabling life lived abundantly. Today, moreover, the context is global. A lifestyle that became common in Europe, North America, Japan, and a few other pockets of the world in the twentieth century is going global in the new century, with countries like China and India joining the 16% of the world's population that consume 80% of global resources. Our Christian faith demands contextualization in a global community. Otherwise its good news for the poor becomes phony and those who are captives stay in their cages.

A contextualized faith does not just meet the culture where it is. Nor does it adapt itself to a prevailing way of life. As part of the proclamation of the Lord's favor, it is critical. It recognizes that change is required. A contextualized faith is always, almost by definition, non-conformist, in the sense Ben Shahn, in *The Shape of Content*, says that any attempt to be true in a way that has not become stale, conventional and aligned with what refuses to change is nonconformist. Without nonconformity we would not have the Magna Carta, no public education system, no NHS, no science at all, and little religion. And of course there is always resistance to nonconformity's struggle for authenticity and creativity. Shahn says, "It may be a point of great pride to have a Van Gogh on the living room wall, but the prospect of having Van Gogh himself in the living room would put a great many devoted art lovers to rout." The proclamation of the year of the Lord's favor implies an uncomfortable imperative that things must change.

Thirdly, the proclamation of the year of the Lord's favor

is a rhetorical assertion of a new truth overcoming and transcending the resistance of the current state of affairs. The new truth is essentially the vivid biblical truth of metaphor. In the sermon he preached just minutes before his assassination while celebrating Mass, for instance, Archbishop Oscar Romero reminded his congregation of the parable of the grain of wheat from the Gospel of John:

> Those who surrender to the service of the poor through love of Christ will live like the grain of wheat that dies. It only apparently dies. If it were not to die, it would remain a solitary grain. The harvest comes because of the grain that dies. We know that every effort to improve society, above all when society is so full of injustice and sin, is an effort that God blesses; that God wants; that God demands of us.

Romero uses the metaphor of life as the seed that has died to interpret the concrete experience of the people, which often enough includes death. And he makes it clear that what the Church is experiencing, like what assassinated Civil Rights movement workers had experienced in the States, is the proper vocation of Christian witness. This is what the metaphor of the grain of wheat does. Faithful disciples whose eyes have been opened will share the experience of Jesus, both the suffering and the blessing. The proclamation of blessing for those whose lives are shaped like the grain of wheat asserts a higher truth than the fact of the death squads, and tells us where we need to stand:

> In less than three years, more than fifty priests have been attacked, threatened, calumniated. Six are already martyrs – they were murdered. Some have been tortured and others expelled [from the country]. Nuns have also been persecuted. The archdiocesan radio station and educational insti-

> tutions that are Catholic or of a Christian inspiration have been attacked, threatened, intimidated, even bombed. Several parish communities have been raided. If all this has happened to persons who are the most evident representatives of the Church, you can guess what has happened to ordinary Christians, to the campesinos, catechists, lay ministers, and to the ecclesial base communities. There have been threats, arrests, tortures, murders, numbering in the hundreds and thousands... But it is important to note why [the Church] has been persecuted. Not any and every priest has been persecuted, not any and every institution has been attacked. That part of the Church has been attacked and persecuted that put itself on the side of the people and went to the people's defense. Here again we find the same key to understanding the persecution of the Church: the poor.

Such proclamation transforms us. In Acts, when Paul is preaching to the cultured, learnèd Athenians, the resurrection is referred to as "this new teaching" (Acts 17:19). The only other place in the New Testament that refers to "new teaching" is in reference to Jesus' first act of ministry in Mark, when the healing of a man possessed is referred to as new teaching – teaching not like that of the scribes and the learning by rote memorization that merely reproduces the past, but as transformation and liberation from oppression, the kind of teaching Paulo Freire has described in *Pedagogy of the Oppressed*. Luke may very well have had the phrase from Mark. Resurrection is neither just a doctrine to be defended against its educated detractors nor an interesting idea to be mulled over in a Wednesday night Bible study, but the proclamation of a reality to be lived and by its experience to be changed.

So the proclamation of the year of the Lord's favor becomes not some comforting fiction to help those who live in fear cope with a world they don't like, but in fact a disclosure of the truth that lies obscured and denied by such fictions. My writing here is an attempt to embody the spirit of such proclamation as disclosure of truth.

Advent 1 C: "Be alert"

Luke 21:25–36

"Be on guard," Jesus says in Luke 21, "so that your hearts are not weighed down with dissipation and drunkenness and the worries of this life, and that day catch you unexpectedly, like a trap."

Why are we always caught so unprepared? Why do we bury our heads in the sand, almost as if this were a characteristic of our species? In a 2004 *Wall Street Journal* article Stephen Roach, the chief economist at Morgan Stanley, said the USA was heading for an economic Armageddon, and that that served as a warning to other nations unavoidably tied to the world's largest economy, like ours.

America, Roach said, needed to import $2.6 billion in cash every working day to finance its current account deficit with the rest of the world. That's not small change. That is an amazing 80% of the entire world's net savings. Household debt accounted for 85% of the American economy, and householders were spending record amounts of their disposable income on interest payments. Roach said America is living in a "debt bubble" of record proportions, and predicted a spectacular wave of bankruptcies coming in the not too distant future that would carry the rest us along with them.

Were any of these debt-burdened households worried? Probably not. They wielded their credit cards that Christmas season as always, shopping as if there will always be a tomorrow, while their bankers were getting rich selling sub-prime mortgages. It all seemed to come as such a surprise when the crash finally came a few years later. And it wasn't just debt that did it. As we now know, after the Lehman Brothers bankruptcy in 2008, the financial collapse was largely driven by the kind of forces Jeff Madrick describes in *Age of Greed: The Triumph of*

Finance and the Decline of America, 1970 to the Present.

I don't think any church can see the future any better than the national economies do that got caught up in the debt crisis. I once looked after a particularly down-and-out church in Chicago. They didn't have a minister. I got a seminarian with a lot of savvy to take the services, and I ran the meetings. It was in one of the roughest neighborhoods in the city. The local street gang used to hang out on the corner in front of the church. They had business cards printed up with the church's address on them.

This church's survival was such an anxious issue that elders' meetings could get like dog fights. Everyone had a different idea of what to do, and differences were strong. At one point disagreements across the table virtually reached the level of shouting matches. I banged my fist hard against the table. The coffee cups jumped at least a centimeter. Everything became quiet. I told them that from now on no one would speak unless they were first recognized by the chair. Only one person would speak at a time. And once you spoke you couldn't speak again until everyone else had had a chance to speak. It all ran smoothly for at least half an hour, and then I had to assert my authority as chair of the meeting once more.

I was at my wits' end. Somehow, I managed to find a professional in conflict resolution who had had some church experience – I think his uncle had been a minister – who agreed to come work with us without charge. We used the backs of campaign posters left over from a recent mayoral election instead of flipchart paper, and posted these on the walls all around the church hall. The upshot of the evening was that after everyone had a chance to say where they were coming from and what their ideas were and write all this up on the big sheets of paper, we recognized that we were all moving in the same direction. It was a watershed for the church. We learned to work together, and explore strategies slowly and carefully.

The magnitude of what the church faced came clear one

Christmas Eve during the sharing of intercessory prayers. We heard about the corner shop owner up the street who had been shot, about a teenage boy connected to the church who had been knifed, about a thirteen-year-old girl who had been gang raped, about evictions and addictions and a wide company of desperation. This was a church that could not wave these problems away with a credit card or numb its conscience with seasonal sentimentality. Its unprotected vision gave it no choice but to be embedded in heart-wrenching circumstances.

Their world was very different from the affluent suburban neighborhood we see depicted, for instance, in *Home Alone*, a Christmas-season movie which gains its emotional power from the sense in which such wealthy communities see themselves under siege. The happy ending of the movie generally proves true in experience. Affluent neighborhoods are generally safer. The poorer the community, the more violence is simply normal. And it's not just gang violence. Chicago police shoot six people a month, killing one a fortnight. Rich neighborhoods, like rich nations, have the power to expel and punish what other neighborhoods must simply suffer.

The Church, for those I was serving, was like the Ark riding on rough seas, yet to see the rainbow. Marieke and I will never forget how at the end of the service, though it had been a midnight service, they didn't want to go home. So we kept singing carol after carol. We used up all the carols in the hymn book, then sang others we knew by heart. Finally, at the very end, we sang *Happy Birthday* to Jesus, and then we held hands and had the charge and blessing. Go in peace into this good night to serve the Lord.

That was the last Christmas before we moved to Wales. The little church on that rough Chicago street corner died itself a few years later, unable to sustain its life against such odds, its death unnoticed by the mania described by Stephen Roach of a world pursuing an unsustainable dream of affluence.

But its death did not invalidate its witness. They lived with integrity, honestly and as faithfully as they could. "Faith is the assurance of things hoped for," we read in Hebrews, "the conviction of things not seen," however, the story actually ends.

Isn't this what it means to "be on guard" and not be caught unprepared? This kind of witness is certainly a better example of what Jesus meant than what we see in *Home Alone*, a celebration of the affluent community's comic vigilance over what threatens it. In *Home Alone* such vigilance can symbolize what divides us, what ghettoizes poverty, what blinds us to suffering. When Jesus calls us to "be on guard" we can trust that he desires us to guard against just such a self-focus.

Here in this Chicago street corner church was a community whose nerves were raw and exposed to a world most Christians have the luxury to avoid. Their faith was no greater and their resources were far fewer than what you find in other churches. But they created light where there was darkness as best as they could. And that is enough for me. I recall a small poem by Tagore: "Faith is the bird / that feels the light / and sings / while the night is still dark." Even if the dawn never seems to come.

That is all anyone can ever ask of a Christian community. We are not asked to get into the Christmas spirit. We are not asked to light our candles with the height of liturgical formality. We are not asked to push back the dark with rich feasting and spending more than we earn – these are simply the distractions that turn our hearts from their proper focus and lead us to be caught unprepared at a time of crisis. Nor are we asked to hide from death. We are called to be as faithful as we can, lest a time of trial catch us unprepared. It's not a seasonal thing. Luke's Jesus asks people to "take up their cross daily" (Luke 9:23) as a way of life.

Advent 2 C: "Speaking out"

Luke 3:1–6

By "baptism" John means repentance.

It is interesting, in light of this traditional Advent theme, that David Cameron and George Osborn and the rest of them are so unrepentant, so determined to stay the course with their cuts, despite so much resistance and upheaval, not only here in Britain but across Europe. It's not just the cuts that get up my nose. 77% of the budget deficit is being recovered from public expenditure cuts and benefit cuts. Only 23% comes from tax increases, more than half of which is the increase in VAT, hitting the poor the hardest, none of it aimed at the folk on the *Sunday Times* Rich List. The wealth of the people on this list increased by £155 billion over the last three years, enough to pay off the entire deficit in one go. No wonder the posh boys want to stay the course. Rowan Williams says David Cameron's Big Society rhetoric is "designed to conceal a deeply damaging withdrawal of the state from its responsibilities to the most vulnerable."

Luke begins this section of his Gospel introducing John the Baptist by giving us a roster of those who were determined to stay the course in the political and religious institutions of the day. We are in the fifteenth year of the reign of Tiberius Caesar, Luke says. Judea is in the hands of a petty but ruthless Italian bureaucrat named Pontius Pilate. Herod Antipas, son of Herod the Great, rules under the patronage of Rome over the Galilee. Philip, his brother, rules the Golan Heights, and Lysanius, Luke says, rules the Gentile territory of what is now Lebanon. History is full of puppet alliances like this. I'm reminded of Franklin Delano Roosevelt's comment about Nicaragua's dictator, "Somoza may be a son of a bitch, but he's our son of a bitch." Then Luke mentions the high priest Caiaphas and his elderly father-in-law Annas, who calls the shots from behind the scenes.

The Temple itself is basically under the patronage of Rome, dependent for the large part of its funding on the patronage of the provincial government. The Temple institution was so corrupt that the remarks Jesus made about its coming collapse were no great prophecy.

This is how Luke begins his introduction to John the Baptist, placing him in a particular location at a particular historical moment, in a political context. Tiberius Caesar is determined to stay the course. Those under him and those obligated to him are determined to stay the course to protect their own positions. But now, verse 2, the word of God comes to John, a specific word with a specific meaning in a specific historical context. Repent, he says. Change course.

Those who think repentance is only an individual change of heart that has nothing to do with the shape of the world, with politics, with society, with the shape of the Church as a whole as well as the individual Christian life, simply do not understand the Gospel. It's not easy to change directions, to start living in a new way, when all the powers and authorities around you are determined to stay the course. These are the powers that control the world you live in, the way it works, the ways its institutions behave, and its values sink into the dark corners of your soul like a warm dose of polonium-210 and take over who you are, or, rather, who you used to be. You are trapped, compromised, your very heart is occupied like Palestine then and now by powers from outside. You want to sing that Iona song, "summon out what I shall be," but the world that owns you keeps pulling you back. Sin possesses you, and is determined to stay the course. You are part of a world that builds super casinos, a world that turns a blind eye to HIV/AIDS, a world that invades Iraq, a world where those who control our money and whose collective greed is more responsible than anything else for our global financial crisis continue to pay themselves obscene bonuses, a world that calls you to stay the course and fills you with guilt if you don't, a terrifying world of Trident missiles. That world lives inside you as part of what drives you.

Michael Hampson, in a book called *Last Rites: The End of the Church of England,* writes of clergy bombarded by a fantasy that the Church is on the brink of revival and renewal, if not last year then this year or the next. Like political leaders in our own day say about Afghanistan, the Church is saying that victory is just around the corner, even while it is surrounded by the evidence for terminal decline. We are trapped by a vision of staying the course, and anyone who dissents from that vision is disloyal.

John says turn around, change course, and be liberated from what is possessing you.

Our translation says we are "forgiven", and you think that means your personal faults and failings are simply set aside with a pat on the head and forgotten. But the word used here, *aphesis* in Greek, carries the sense that to be forgiven is to be liberated from what has entrapped you, in the sense that Jesus, reading from Isaiah in Luke 4, says the Lord has sent him to "proclaim release [*aphesis*] to the captives." What imprisons you? It may be the pressure from the "scribes" to always have the right answers and never think of imaginative alternatives. It may be the pressure to play the expected gender role. It may be the pressure of our generation's addiction to petrol or the pressure to put corporate profit before human need. To be forgiven is to be liberated to live in a new kind of world. Here we find the seeds of the kingdom.

Luke, following the Gospel of Mark, quotes Isaiah, speaking of a voice that cries out in the wilderness, "Prepare the way of the Lord." Then he adds the rest of the Isaiah that Mark doesn't have. "Every valley shall be raised, and every mountain and hill be made low, the crooked shall be made straight, and the rough places smooth; and all flesh shall see the salvation of God."

The leveling Isaiah had in mind was a way home from exile, a summoning out from captivity of what we shall be when our

God puts his seal on our hearts and lives in us. Such a path is a way to a new world, the kind of world in which the Lord brings down the powerful from their thrones and lifts up the lowly. Such leveling of the social landscape is central to Luke's Gospel.

It doesn't always work so neatly in real life. Maybe we can see rough places made smooth in the way *The Sun* took credit for ending the "hated" pasty tax, with George Osborne admitting that he had "listened to *Sun* readers." *The Daily Mail* declared victory against the secret courts, with Kenneth Clarke saying: "*The Mail* has done a service to the public interest." Perhaps a level, open democracy creates welcome opportunities for advocacy and pressure. Our government's U-turns, which Labor pounces on as revealing what a complete shambles we're in, are like acts of repentance, the recognition that mid-course changes are needed to correct bad earlier decisions. Is this the kind of leveling-out Luke is talking about? Is this the kind of repentance John the Baptist is calling for? I remember stopping at a kosher Jewish food shop in Birmingham once, and mentioning to the proprietor that Sainsbury's was now carrying bagels. He said, "Well, they *look* like bagels…"

The problem remains that the pressure isn't just coming from the media but from big money, like the defense industry, construction and banking interests. It may look like democracy, until you consider the weight these powerful interests carry around. As Theodore Roosevelt said in 1906, in relation to his use of the Sherman Antitrust Act in his campaign against monopolies:

> Behind the ostensible government sits enthroned an invisible government owing no allegiance and acknowledging no responsibility to the people. To destroy this invisible government, to befoul the unholy alliance between corrupt business and corrupt politicians is the first task of the statesmanship of the day.

But "statesmanship" has never been able to clear the deck entirely. Real life is a messy business. Nevertheless, that doesn't mean our vocation is to fold our hands and doze off, powerless, in our easy chairs. Christians need to be engaged.

Some people think that Advent is a way of patiently counting the chocolates of our Advent calendars through the days of December, one by one, until we get to Christmas. The idea behind that, I suppose, is to teach good Calvinist children about the ascetic virtue of deferred gratification.

But Advent is more properly about impatience. It is about the courage to see the world as a project gone badly wrong. We catch a vision of how things can be different, and speak out. That's what prepares the way for the Lord. It has nothing to do with the winter solstice. It's not even a matter of remembering the birthday of Jesus. It is a matter of our own discipleship and our own root-and-branch renewal that enables Christ to be born right here and now, today, and to be alive in our midst and in who we are.

Advent 3 C: "Cinderella"

Luke 3:7–20

Imagine the story of John the Baptist as a winter-season British Pantomime.

The people of Judea are coming down to the Jordan River like a gathering of ugly sisters determined to squeeze into the glass slipper. Why? Because, as children of Abraham, they assume the privilege of marrying the prince will be theirs, and that the slipper will fit. The image these children of Abraham present here is that of the ridiculous, self-centered twits we see in the pantomime's ugly sisters.

The ugly sisters are usually played by a couple of men. I saw a very funny school production once in which one of the sisters actually had a beard, and of course their frocks had to be in horrid bad taste. They looked like Mick Jagger prancing about in a frock in that 1969 Hyde Park concert, hardly the lady you would want to have as your sister.

What is so funny about the two sisters is that they see themselves as paragons of beauty, elegance, charm and wit, the way most people like to see themselves. They, like the children of Abraham who come down to the Jordan River, seem to represent that chronic self-absorption that is such a significant part of our human nature. This is what we are like.

John the Baptist calls them sons of snakes. No, we're not, they protest. And the congregation responds, O yes, you are! O no, we're not, they say. O yes, you are! And John the Baptist says, "You are sons of snakes! You call yourselves sons of Abraham… why, God could make sons of Abraham out of paving stones!"

John the Baptist becomes a kind of Magic Mirror for the people of Judea who come down to the Jordan to be baptized. They want to hear how beautiful they are. The kind of forgiveness they want is a nice little re-affirmation of who they are, a smile and a pat on the head. Here is what they say:

Mirror, mirror, on the wall,
Who's the fairest of them all?
Am I not pretty, slim and slight,
The perfect image of Snow White?

John the Baptist answers back:

No, you're not, you silly fool.
I thought at first you were a mule!

The second ugly sister pushes the first out of the way. Who is the fairest of them all? she asks the Mirror. And the Baptist says:

Your looks are hardly worth a toot,
The world knows you are no beaut.
What really counts is bearing fruit.
A fruitless tree we shall uproot,
Burn it, toss it down the chute.

The first ugly sister now shoulders the second out of the way.

Then I'm the prettiest; yes, it's me!
That's the truth I want to see!

But John the Baptist says:

No, no, no, no. That is not true!
If anyone, it is not you!
It's certain now you have no clue.
The proof of beauty's what you do!

So the ugly sisters look at each other, and then they look back at the Magic Mirror and ask, simultaneously, both of them together, "So what are we to do?"

A Methodist minister friend of mine once celebrated their Methodist circuit-riding heritage by bringing a real horse into the church one Sunday morning. It was a stallion. He says the next time he does this he is going to use a pantomime horse, two guys in a horse suit. He was a city boy, not a country boy. He didn't think about what can happen to stallions in an otherwise uneventful Sunday morning worship service.

What John the Baptist did down there at the Jordan River in those days was just as disruptive as bringing an excitable stallion into a Methodist Sunday morning worship service, or the zany, irreverent comedy of Pantomime itself, which has no respect whatsoever for the concept of propriety.

Pantomime, with its rudeness and its disrespect for everything from the dignity of age to gender identity itself, represents what cultural historians call a pressure valve for the pent-up tension of a conservative society. Spitting Image and Monty Python once served a similar function, but British Pantomime has formed the more enduring institution. The cultural role played by Pantomime is to deflate the puffed up pretensions of the powerful, to bring down to earth a pompous, hierarchical, class-bound society that demands conformity and stiff obedience, the kind of society that finds its natural expression in the way children get yelled at in school, or, in former years, beaten with sticks. Pantomime is like a January pressure-release valve that allows us to re-enter the world of social control in February, tension temporarily relieved in harmless play. Of course the big difference between Pantomime and what John the Baptist is doing down there at the Jordan River is that he wants real change, not a pressure valve to allow and so reinforce a world that will not change.

But consider for a moment that the story of John the Baptist is more like a Pantomime than we might think. Where might we find here a character like Cinderella?

I think everyone recognizes that, spiritually, the Cinderella of the Pantomime is that unrecognized beauty within themselves that finally finds someone who will cherish it for what it is. We're not just describing the primordial archetypes of depth psychology here. Theologians speak of the unrecognized beauty that lies within each of us as the image of God, or the face of Christ, a beauty that we ourselves have often failed to recognize, a beauty which has become disfigured, impoverished, tattered and abused not only by the bullying stepsisters of this world, so to speak, but even by ourselves, by what we do or fail to do. Throughout the Gospel of Luke we see Jesus finding the hidden beauty of rejected and diminished people, lifting it out and celebrating it. His Gospel is full of such people.

John's call to repentance is a call for us to cherish that beauty hidden within us, and so begin living differently. We are invited to be liberated from all that we have allowed to entrap us and bind us, and so become those through whom the presence of God can shine. We are those whose discipleship bears fruit. We are re-born as God's own daughters and sons.

For Christians, I think Christmas is less the birthday of Jesus than it is the occasion of our own re-birth in this sense.

Advent 4 C: "Getting local"

Luke 1:39–45

My first Christmas in Wales, in 1988, I presided at nine carol services. As the new minister on a sprawling council estate, serving three churches, I was in demand. Each church had its own carol service, and then there were the women's organizations, the schools and the clubs. It was exhausting, and enough to put one off carol singing for life, as I thought at the time. There had been nothing like this in Chicago.

Though formally the carol services have their origin in the stately, late Victorian practice at King's College Chapel, Cambridge, their popularity reaches back to their pre-Christian roots, like the popular mid-winter pantomimes with their cross-dressing and madcap, plotless ribaldry.

Curious about the way Christmas was practiced in Wales, I attended a carol service held at St Fagan's, the open-air National History Museum of Wales on the grounds of St Fagan's Castle. The museum consists of an expansive collection of reconstructed farm buildings, miners' cottages, shops and dwellings – a broad sweep of Welsh history, brought together from all around Wales. The carol service was held in a Unitarian church from the eighteenth century, Penrhiw Chapel, which originally stood in Dre-fach Felindre, Carmarthenshire.

The small building was packed shoulder-to-shoulder that night, and, with no electric lighting, it was dark. Those who thought ahead brought electric torches to read the carol sheets. Crammed into a corner of the upstairs gallery without a torch, I sang along from memory as best I could. I had the feeling of being deeply embedded among the people.

My last Christmas in Chicago hadn't been like this. As a local minister, I had been a member of the Northtown Chamber of Commerce on Chicago's far north side. Our president organized a promotional event for the Christmas shopping season in one of the stores. It was attended by a photographer from the local paper and less than a dozen businessmen, mostly Jewish, as this was a predominantly Jewish neighborhood. Even the one dressed in a Santa suit was Jewish. I remember him complaining that being Jewish was all about suffering from heartburn. Other than those of us who had to be there, no one from the general public was in attendance.

Our president had arranged to give a large Christmas box of gifts donated by local merchants to Northtown's 'neediest family'. How they selected this young woman and her four skinny kids I don't know. She was a member of the local Catholic church. Maybe the parish priest had recommended her. In any case, she was very grateful, and she and her children sang a couple of songs for us. This was Christmas in America.

For all its earthy, pre-Christian spirit, what I found in Wales seemed to connect more authentically to a people's voice, the kind of voice Mary embodies for us. In the "Magnificat" Mary sings from deep within the longing heart of her people about a hope that has found a fulfillment which is palpable and local:

> He has scattered the proud in the thoughts of their hearts.
> He has brought down the powerful from their thrones,
> and lifted up the lowly.
> He has filled the hungry with good things,
> and sent the rich away empty.

Leaving the Unitarian chapel that dark December night, I came across a group of serious-looking young men who were part of the night's celebrations. They were carrying what they call the "Mari Lwyd" (the Grey Mare), a horse's skull covered with a sheet and decorated with colorful ribbons, the sheet long enough to cover the operator, who clicked the horse's jaws together using a wooden pulley. Now this was definitely a relic of pre-Christian

Wales, and frightening to behold. But learning more, I discovered its association with question-and-answer games, calling around the village homes seeking to share in mid-winter hospitality, joyful feasting and festive drinking. The Mari Lwyd has pretty much died out, except among folklore societies. But confronting a re-enacted tradition like this on a dark winter night can nevertheless take you deeper into the life of a people, where among memories of miners' strikes and steel-workers' unions you can discern the still-warm embers of a people's hope, that kind of hope Mary had, of whom her cousin Elizabeth said, "Blessed is she who believed that there would be a fulfillment of what was spoken to her by the Lord."

Christmas Eve C: "The Night Before Christmas"

Luke 2:1–14

Cultural historians tell us that it was the poem *The Night Before Christmas*, published in 1823, that was more responsible than anything else for the way Christmas focuses on children.

A Christmas where children's dreams of sugar plums are indulged by cheerful capitalistic elves does not come very close to the Bible's story of Christmas. While we work hard and drive ourselves into debt to conform to the world of *The Night Before Christmas*, the Bible tells a story that is actually more true to life. Here is the story of children in an adult world where homeless families are turned out by hotels booked for seasonal indulgence, where children are held in detention centers when asylum petitions are turned down, or die as victims of political upheaval. Over half the world's refugees today are children.

Conscious that the Bible's version of the Christmas story continues to be the more accurate version twenty centuries later, we gather at church on Christmas Eve in solidarity with the darkness in the lives of today's children, orphaned by or themselves dying from AIDS, for instance. While in Britain we all become children at Christmas, singing carols, dreaming of presents under the tree, escaping into a seasonal innocence, in Africa children who have lost their parents are forced to become adults, caring for their families, struggling for survival. How do we get in touch with their darkness? How do we get in touch with the darkness of children who are abused, on the run, victims of cutbacks in our social services budget, preyed upon by merchants, their lives crippled by our mad rush to war against those whose oil reserves we so desperately need for ourselves? It was into such darkness that Christ was born, not the dreamy Bing Crosby mid-winter darkness they try to sell us, but that darker darkness from which the forgotten cry out in hope. We gather on Christmas Eve not in nostalgia but to learn to hope.

I do not think the tinseled, nostalgic lights of our winter festivities will teach us to hope. Christmas calls us to get connected with those who hunger, with those who thirst for righteousness, with the refugee who longs for a place of safety, with the peacemaker struggling to build an alternative to a world locked in conflict. Dylan Thomas, in *A Child's Christmas in Wales*, spoke nostalgically of the season's "snow-felted darkness." Here we speak of a different kind of darkness. And until we touch such darkness, and discover the light that shines from that darkness, we will never really know what it means to hope or be a people of hope. We will never recognize Christmas when it comes. We will be condemned to a flat, shopping mall landscape without meaning and without passion, where hope rarely rises above the lottery or the middle class toys waiting for us under the tree. We need to learn a deeper hope than what we have known.

The night that comes before Christmas is important; in the same sense that you cannot have Easter without moving through Good Friday, there is no birth of a Christ child without the experience of inns that close their doors. Paul says at one point (Philippians 3:10) that he wants to share in the sufferings of Christ, even in his death, that through such experience he might know the power of Christ's resurrection. So we must seek the darkness that comes before Christmas.

Christmas Day C: "Off to join the world"

John 1:1–14

Saxophone player Jimmy Jewell went on tour with Gary Glitter's Rock 'n' Roll Circus back in the early 1980s. The show was dying everywhere. Jimmy hadn't been paid in weeks, so he got up in the early hours of the morning one night, raided the petty cash box, and skipped off. He left a note saying, "Goodbye, cruel circus. I'm off to join the world!"

The flight from circus to world is the trajectory of incarnation. In Philippians 2, Paul invites us to think like Jesus. He could have been somebody. He could have been a trapeze artist, a lion tamer; he could have ridden magnificent stallions standing barefoot on their backs as they raced around the center ring to the roar of an approving crowd. But he chose instead to be ordinary, to be a servant, to throw his lot in with the despised and the dying. He decided to join the world. That's what the incarnation is all about.

Christians need to understand that the incarnation is not a matter of biology but of commitment, of deciding where they are going to stand. In the annual Christmas play one year, the youth group at City United Reformed Church put 'God the Father' and 'God the Son' on stage, lounging amid the clouds of heaven. When the Second Person of the Trinity poignantly consented to enter into the painful reality of our ordinary world, there was something that gripped us emotionally. We had been there ourselves, at the point of decision. The pantomime make-believe of the literal surface faded into the background. This was reality. Our own reality. We knew what it meant to commit ourselves to joining the world, or could at least imagine what it might mean.

The real incarnation takes place in moments like the Garden of Gethsemane, when Jesus knelt to pray, "Not my will, but yours be done." It's what we pray every time we pray the Lord's

Prayer. Your will be done on earth. Through us. Maybe the Christmas story puts this prayer into narrative form so that children can act it out before they reach the point, as adults, when they must live it out.

The Word became flesh and lived among us, says the Gospel of John. The word becomes flesh in Jesus the same way it takes on flesh in any of us, when God's will becomes human act. As Christians we say this is a decisive moment, perhaps the decisive moment in the lives of all Christians. We along with Jesus are also called to be sons and daughters of God, born, as he was, "not of blood or of the will of the flesh or of the will of a man, but of God." The decision is ours: Are we going to go on tour with Gary Glitter's Rock 'n' Roll Circus, or are we going to join the world?

What do adult Christians 'believe' about Christmas? Isn't what we believe in what Mary sang about, the importance of justice, of compassion, of a Lord who scatters the proud and exalts those of low degree?

Whether you do or whether you don't believe in the virgin birth, for instance, doesn't change how much money people get for picking coffee beans in Ethiopia. But if you believe that God is on the side of fair trade, and you put that belief into action, then what people get for picking coffee beans in Ethiopia might actually have a chance of changing, because someone like you has believed that the will of God is important.

Society seems so much more interested in the circus, especially around Christmas time. We hunger for the extravagant spectacle, the heroic acrobatics, the drama, the lights, and a theology to match. Merchants of illusion have found a thousand ways to sell it to us.

Well, I, too, like the circus. But my heart tells me I ought to love the world more. And Christmas invites me to decide.

Christmas 1 C: "Get lost!"

Luke 2:41–52

Picture in your mind's eye the scene in Luke 2, when Joseph and Mary bring the boy Jesus up to Jerusalem: the shoulder-to-shoulder festival crowds, the holiday noise, the street entertainers, stalls lining the narrow streets selling fast food and souvenirs, everyone dressed up for celebration. This was noisy, vibrant Jerusalem celebrating Passover and Jesus was there, aged 12, with his parents and their neighbors from Nazareth.

It's the kind of scene you can imagine losing your kids in, like going to London for the post-Christmas sales. In a Palestinian culture of extended families Mary and Joseph wouldn't worry so much if they hadn't seen their twelve-year-old for a while. Somebody's got him. Everybody belongs to everybody else. Imagine how easy it is going to be to lose your kid. You're halfway home, and suddenly it occurs to you to ask, "Where is Tommy?" Mary is a whole day away from Jerusalem on her way back to Nazareth when she realizes Jesus has gone missing. "Where is Jesus?" she says in a panic.

In *The Wall Street Journal* there was an article about a man named Richard Elggren, a dentist, who lost his son in a crowd of shoppers. He had no idea what his son was wearing, and had never thought about what to do in such a situation. Elggren decided to do something in case this ever happened again. He implanted a computer chip in one of his son's teeth that had all the information about who he was and where he lived, so that if he ever got lost again he could easily be found.

Imagine living in a society where no one ever got lost. Here is Tom Arthur, National Security Number **-**-**-*, American Social Security Number ***-**-****, Lloyd's bank pin number ****, password ******, username *****@)****.btclick.com, mother's maiden name **** with no 'e', secret number for my Coop bank account ****, and my Sainsbury's loyalty card tells them what I buy, and how they can do a better job of fine-tuning their marketing strategies to help me buy more of what I don't need.

Computers track the organizations you belong to, the meetings you attend, what you buy at the grocery store. The unique image of your iris is on file, there is a barcode implanted in your teeth, on your forehead, sewn into your clothing. You are tethered to your e-mail and your mobile phone. You never have to get lost. You are forever tied to the world of your parents. You never really have to leave home, no matter how far you wander; you never have to be a stranger or experience disorientation, never have to be lost. Everybody speaks English. Imagine how comforting it would be, never having to leave the security of your mother's protective presence.

Of course sometimes being lost is not a bad thing to be. What was Jesus doing, there in the Temple? Have you ever been lost in thought, has being lost in conversation ever transported you into another world? Here was the twelve-year-old Jesus preparing for his Bar Mitzvah, honing his understanding, lost in argument, carried away from ordinary concerns into a world of deep meaning and even deeper commitment. If this is being lost, it's not a bad place to be.

There is also the sense of being lost in terms of really leaving home, of coming of age, of breaking ties. This is what begins to happen to you when you are about 12 years old. You begin to embrace disorientation from what is too predictable and too familiar as a kind of prelude to an orientation to something that is new and different.

In this sense the experience of being lost is like conversion, like all experiences of transformation that begin with a feeling of disorientation, of feeling lost, of vertigo, of losing your bearings, conscious that something is missing here, and even while you are still at home you begin feeling more and more like an exile, like someone who doesn't belong anymore, a refugee, on the run.

You long for compassion in government or moral integrity in the workplace and they tell you that you are naïve and weak. You want fair play and honesty in commerce or even in the Church and they accuse you of holding to pointless scruples. Get real. Unable to distinguish between spin and reality you call for truth and accountability and they say you lack the manly attributes required to wage war on terror. After a while home doesn't look like home any more. You are lost.

Notice the symbolic fabric of this story. What festival is it that is being celebrated in Jerusalem? Passover! How long does Mary take to find her son again? Look at verse 46 – three days. Is that significant? Is this a resurrection story, the way all conversion and coming of age and leaving home stories are resurrection stories?

This story of Jesus in the Temple raises some compelling questions. It may be that those are really lost who have never left home. It may be that we are never really found until we have first become lost.

It's one of the hardest things for anyone to do, and one of the hardest things for any church to do, to let go of the mothering familiarity of where we have been in order to take up the new life of where we need to be.

When does the predictability of the old become so uncomfortable that we are ready and even eager to risk all – painful disorientation, suffering, even the cross – for something new? Paul, in Philippians, says the things of his former life do nothing but hold him back. They are a pile of crap, he says, literally translated (*skubalon*, Philippians 3:8), compared to what he has gained in Christ.

So here's a New Year's wish for you: "Get lost!" and do so boldly enough that you might also know what it means to be truly found, not by what you have been but by what you shall be, and for the first time in your life you will discover what it truly means to be home, and about your father's business.

Christmas 2 C: "Going Postal"

John 1:10–18

There are two ways Christians have of understanding the place of God in events like the tsunami of Boxing Day 2004. One is that God, as an all-powerful God, is for some inscrutable reason responsible for this disaster.

My first acquaintance with Christians who think this way was in 1953 when my school teacher, Mrs. Dieter, read to us a letter from her cousin in Holland, who said that the high seas that breached the dykes and caused so many deaths was God's vengeance on a sinful people. Mrs. Dieter said this was poppycock and that we shouldn't think of God in this way.

Another way Christians say that God is present in disasters like this is to say that God is present in the compassion of the human heart that responds to situations like this.

These two possible Christian positions were represented on Radio 4 by a Muslim on the one hand and a Hindu on the other. The Muslim said this disaster was the inscrutable will of God, who was somehow testing us in these events.

The Hindu interviewed said we need to see God in the human compassion that responds. We live in a chaotic world with regularly recurring political upheaval, domestic violence and natural disasters. How do we respond to these things as religious people except by the God-given mercy, love and sense of justice that dwells in our hearts?

In our Gospel lesson we are reminded of that part of the Christmas story that says the Word becomes flesh in us. In verse 12 we are told that all who receive God's Word are given the power to become children of God, sons and daughters of God, brothers and sisters of Jesus of Nazareth. Verse 13: we are born, not of blood or of the will of the flesh or of a human father, but of God.

This is the kind of birth that comes to us when we sing that Iona song, "Through our lives and by our prayers, your kingdom come." A bigger agenda than our own will take over our identity. In such moments God's will becomes our will. I think of a verse from Ephesians: "Now to him who by the power at work within us is able to accomplish abundantly far more than all we can ask or imagine, to him be glory in the Church and in Christ Jesus to all generations, forever and ever."

John Calvin once wrote that the will of God does not come like the dew from heaven. Nor, we can assume, does it come in the form of a tsunami. God's will is accomplished by the hands of the faithful community.

All the 2004 tsunami stories of helicopters and boats reaching desperately remote villages and frantic efforts to reach populations not yet contacted were all stories of something bigger than us happening through us, as if God's will for life was becoming enfleshed in us.

Lists of names posted on the Internet, DNA samples and dental records, photographs posted in Sri Lankan post offices represent a need to connect with what had been broken. A camera was found on a Phi Phi Island beach. The snapshots it contained of young women on holiday in Thailand were posted on the net. There were thousands of little stories like this.

And the voices of survivors telling us that aid was still not coming quickly enough or efficiently enough were crying out across the thousands of miles between us to overcome what separates us.

From the joy of the father at the return home of the Prodigal Son to Paul's mission among the Gentiles, and all the way back to God's compassion for the slaves in Egypt, the Bible is about repairing broken connections. There is a brilliant story about someone who repairs connections in Terry Pratchett's novel, *Going Postal*. It is a story about a man who is given responsibility for reorganizing a post office overflowing with undelivered letters.

What is significant is that this man's previous life has been characterized by an extraordinary *lack* of responsibility, by laziness and even criminality. Now he has a chance to redeem himself.

There was no end to the letters, Pratchett writes. "They filled every room of the building and spilled out into the corridors. The postmaster's office was unusable because it was twenty feet deep in letters. Whole corridors were blocked off. Cupboards had been stuffed full of them. Just to open a door incautiously would be to be buried in an avalanche of yellowing envelopes."

Why had these letters never been delivered? There always seemed to be other priorities, other pressing responsibilities, like keeping the ink wells topped up with ink, or any of the multiple details of our own overwhelmed lives, all the myriad petty details and responsibilities that keep us from being neighbors, that keep us so boxed up in our own little worlds, separated, unconnected and alone.

Soon enough the undelivered mail starts to cry out audibly to the new postmaster, desperately attempting to make their hidden contents known. "Deliver us," they cry. "Deliver us." "Deliver us."

Epiphany C: "Losing the plot"

Isaiah 60:1–6; Matthew 2:1–12

When I was a kid my parents used to wake me up every morning saying, "Rise and shine!" After undergoing training for the ministry, I was able to call back, "Isaiah 60, verse 1!"

These words in Isaiah were spoken to a people who had been living in exile, living for two generations in what is today Iraq, until, one day, the possibility of a return home is announced.

"Rise and shine," Isaiah says. These words were a great encouragement for a people who would return home to find a bombed out Jerusalem, its economy in ruins. Imagine what it must have felt like to sift through the rubble, with all the dreams you'd been telling each other of what it could be like turning now to ashes in your mouth. This is reality. This is no longer the dream.

But Isaiah attempts to keep the dream alive. Isaiah not only assures Israel that Jerusalem will return to its former glory, but that it will be even better. Nations and kings will queue up eager to trade, verse 3. It will be like the regeneration of Cardiff Bay, only more spectacular.

The world's wealth will pour into a revived Jerusalem, and its new economic and military muscle will enable it to become a major player in controlling global shipping and mineral resources and oil reserves. This is the triumph of globalized capital. A multitude of camels will come, verse 6, bearing gold and frankincense. Nations will bring their wealth, and those that refuse, those that don't bring their wealth to Jerusalem will be brutally destroyed, verse 12. The story Isaiah tells evokes a perennial dream of loss restored.

A colleague and I were having a conversation once about how our churches dream for a restoration of their former Victorian glory, when Christendom and Empire seemed to be so indissolubly one. My friend said, "The reality is that most of them will die." But they can't face that. That's what drives the hunger for the past.

Some churches present the appearance of restored glory by trading in the images of power and success and domination that so captivate the public imagination. The theology is still Victorian, empire-building stuff about glory and majesty and power, while the music is contemporary, upbeat, triumphant. For people with diminished hope, it has a certain appeal, transporting them out of the real world. People like to be part of something big, even if it is only imaginary.

All churches seem to hold on tenaciously to this dream of restored glory, even when their numbers dwindle down to fifty, twenty, ten, sometimes four or five members, unable to face the inexorable reality of death.

We see a similar phenomenon here in Cardiff as a city, hungry to return to the economic boom story of coal and steel days by grasping after the dream of economic recovery. So Cardiff has become a local hub of globalization, with globally-connected financial services, European community funding for development, a world-class rugby stadium, a state-of-the-art performance center for musicals, opera and dance, and one of the strongest retail centers in the UK. Cardiff also knows the spiritual misery that attends any society's transition to a primarily service economy with its armies of minor clerks and crowded call centers. The thick layer of cosmetics covering the cadaverous remains of Cardiff's once vibrant docklands has yielded a society focused largely on entertainment. The big investment has been thrown at facilities catering for those who have too much money to spend, while those who live in what they call Cardiff's "arc of deprivation" find essential services increasingly hard to come by and quality of life increasingly deteriorating. Binge drinking is endemic, and then there are the casinos and the drug pushers and the imported East European sex workers that feed off the new affluence. It's a dream that is also a nightmare.

The promises of Isaiah 60 form the plot of Matthew, chapter 2. The dream pursued here in Matthew's Gospel is ancient, universal and deep seated in the soul. Lost glory will be restored. The three magi in Matthew's Gospel come like Isaiah's tribute-bearing kings bringing their gifts of gold, frankincense and myrrh to the newborn child.

If you believe in the restoration of this sort of power and authority, of course, the first place you go is going to be where the magi went, the palace, the seat of the rich and the famous. So the magi show up at Herod's palace in Jerusalem. But Herod's theologians, perhaps reluctantly, tell them they have been following the wrong plot. It's Bethlehem they want, not Jerusalem. The true biblical hope is not for global domination, not for a return to a lost political and economic glory. Biblical hope is for one who emerges from within the people, one who knows what it means to hunger and thirst for righteousness.

Let's imagine Bethlehem to be as it is today, a West Bank Palestinian village, walled off, access to its olive groves denied, a place where, according to the *Independent* one Christmas season, babies die because of an economic collapse brought on by Israeli occupation. Here, among the defeated, is where we find those who have the ability to hope for a new and different world. Our first impulse may be to look in Herod's palace for a messiah, but it is as if someone asks, as we will hear it asked later, in Luke's Gospel, "Why do you seek the living among the dead?"

They feel awkward, now, inappropriately overdressed in their fine silks and gold brocade as they enter the humble shack, almost ashamed. One by one they leave their gifts, worthless now in their sight. Except for the myrrh, the funeral spice, which hadn't been on Isaiah's gift list. It must have seemed strangely appropriate now, for one who surely was never going to be a winner. They leave as those to whom much has been given, and from whom much will be required.

We dream of a triumphant Christendom restored to its former glory. Of course we do. It's hard not to. But the Gospel teaches us to live by another story, a story more in keeping with the cross.

Epiphany 2 C: "The guest is host"

Isaiah 62:1–5; John 2:1–11

When Marieke and I got married it was a bit like that last episode of *The Vicar of Dibley*. Did you see it? Geraldine gets married, and all the parish wants a hand in arranging the celebration. This is what happens when a church's minister gets married. Alice Tinker, the dizzy verger, for instance, is to be the maid of honor. She wants to give a Time Lord's flavor to the affair, so she herself dresses as Dr. Who and has the bridesmaids come dressed as Daleks. Geraldine herself, desiring as all ministers do to encourage the ministry of the laity, bites her tongue as they parade their cherished but zany ideas before her. She does her best at being graciously affirmative, but then when they leave she goes to the kitchen to put her head in the oven.

That's the way the church took over things when Marieke and I got married. We lost control of the affair. What we wound up experiencing at their hands was a well-kept secret, a surprise and, fortunately for us, an absolute delight.

And something similar happens here at Cana. Mary and her son Jesus and his friends are guests at the wedding, and when the wine runs out it is Mary who takes over, not the bridegroom. He's lost control. His guests have taken over, and that has made it a very delightful affair indeed.

This is what happens in all good Christian hospitality. The guest becomes our host. The oppressed become our teachers; our consciousness becomes transformed as our lives are given new direction by the needs of our neighbors. In strangers who are hungry, in strangers who are sick or in prison, in strangers who are without shelter, we see the face of Christ. Christ takes over the feasting that we had thought was in our control, and turns it into something far more wonderful than anything we had ever been able to ask for or imagine. "Come, risen Lord," the hymn says, "and deign to be our guest; nay, let us be *your* guests; the feast is thine!" My friend Badri Raina tells me there is a popular saying in Hinduism that makes the point with even greater clarity: "The guest is God."

I think John's readers would have recognized in this wedding banquet story an image of the profound delight that is promised to us in our relationship with God. In Isaiah God is with Israel as a young man is with his bride, intimate, passionately together after extended estrangement. In Jeremiah reconciliation with God is experienced as the mirth of the bridegroom and the joy from the bride. In Matthew the kingdom is imagined as a wedding feast, and in the Book of Revelation God's presence with the people of God is imagined again as a marriage. The scene at Cana is rich with a significance set deeply in Scripture.

So Scripture is no stranger to intimacy. Christians are invited to know God with all the delight in which a newly married couple know one another, or an old, mellowed married couple know one another, for that matter. Everyone knows that Adam knew Eve, Genesis 4:1, in the same way we are invited to know that the Lord is God, Isaiah 37:20, Psalm 46:10, Deuteronomy 4:35, in our full and complete engagement, the totality of our devotion, commitment, delight. Remember how Paul in Romans 12 calls us to worship with such totality of engagement. He wants our very bodies, he says, as a living sacrifice. "Do not be conformed to this world, but be transformed by the renewing of your minds, so that you may discern what is the will of God – what is good and acceptable and perfect." This is how we know God. In the flesh.

My Hebrew professor in seminary, Bob Boling, used to describe the Hebrew word for 'know' as the Hebrew Hokey-pokey – you put your whole self in. And the word used for God's love for us and our love for God is not far distant. Remember how in the prophet Hosea God says "I will love them freely," using a Hebrew verb equally conveying the sense of lovers making love.

The point is, life with God is good news, really good news. It is like a wedding party, grace upon grace.

When I was growing up the table grace my family said together began with, "Come, Lord Jesus, be our guest." Remember that at Emmaus it is in the guest that the forlorn disciples recognize the presence of the risen Christ. Perhaps this is also the way it is for us, when, in the spirit of hospitality, we allow our guests to determine our agenda.

According to the Cana story, which in John launches the beginning of Jesus' ministry, the best wine is served last. This beginning of John's Jesus story looks forward to its end, to what Jesus calls his "hour", his time of crisis, his trial, his crucifixion. The real miracle of this story is not changing water into wine. That's just poetry, of course. The real miracle is that the delight of God's presence is discovered most intimately at the cross. God's shameless intimacy with us, celebrated as a wedding feast, comes so unexpectedly, at the cross, with Christ giving himself to us so completely, so richly, so wonderfully, at his execution. He shares completely in the depths and heights, the length and breadth of what it means to be human. "Consummatum est," he will say then. It's done. It's finished. And so we learn to give ourselves to one another, completely, sharing our journeys in enduring commitment, living compassionately, and so knowing one another, and therefore also God, in delight.

Epiphany 3 C: "Incandescent clarity"

Luke 4:14–20

In April 1967, Martin Luther King Jr. spoke at a meeting of Clergy and Laity Concerned at New York City's Riverside Church about his opposition to the growing war in Vietnam. A year later, he would be assassinated. This is what he said at Riverside Church. He said we are called as Christians to allegiances and loyalties broader and deeper than nationalism and which go beyond our nation's self-defined goals and positions. This is basically what Jesus is saying here in Luke 4. The good news is not just for us, any more than it was just for the respectable members of the Nazareth synagogue. It is for the destitute, the victim, the broken wherever they are. As King said at Riverside Church, "We are called to speak for the weak, for the voiceless, for the victims of our nation and for those it calls 'enemy', for no document from human hands can make these humans any less our brothers and sisters."

No public figure of King's stature had ever spoken so brazenly against their government's war. It was very disorienting. I will never forget how I first heard about opposition to the war. An African American friend arrived at an evening gathering in my apartment in Bloomington, Indiana, grinning widely and carrying a six pack of beer. About an hour later the discussion of the Vietnam War he introduced shifted the atmosphere from its original jovial fellowship to heated debate. After he left, my neighbor and I stayed up through the wee hours in agonized, soul-searching discussion, wrestling with our convictions. He was a somewhat fallen away Mennonite. Both of us had been active in the Civil Rights movement.

People like J. Edgar Hoover, then head of the FBI, had already been hounding King for his civil rights work. King's opposition to the war in Vietnam ignited passionate, intense opposition. It was more than likely that this opposition to the war in Vietnam led to his assassination, not his work for the civil rights of African Americans. This was still in the anti-Communist fever they called the Cold War. The heat of patriotism was intense. But regardless of our attitude toward conservative America's paranoia of a global Communist conspiracy and the domino theory, the idea of opposing our nation's war in Vietnam caught us off foot. We were children of fathers who had fought in what they called "the Good War", after all.

King shared his understanding of how difficult it would be to make such a stand under these circumstances. "Even when pressed by the demands of inner truth," he said, "we do not easily assume the task of opposing our government's policy, especially in time of war." And he spoke of how hard it is to move against all the apathy of conformist thinking that sits within our own souls and in the world we inhabit. He admits that issues like this conflict can be so complex that we risk being mesmerized by uncertainty. "But we must move on," he said. "We must move on."

King challenged the Christian community to discover something at the center of its identity broader than its own flourishing. "Beyond the calling of race or nation or creed," he said, "is this vocation of sonship and brotherhood, and because I believe that the Father is deeply concerned especially for his suffering and helpless and outcast children, I come tonight to speak for them."

Certainly Luke wants us to think that Jesus was condemned to execution for similar convictions. His good news is for the broken victims of all humanity. Jesus will have nothing to do with merely parochial loyalties. God is not coming to rescue Israel as Israel. That may have been the business of the popularly expected Messiah, but Jesus reaches back to something deeper and richer in his people's tradition. This good news Jesus announces is good news for the poor as poor, liberty for the captive as captive, with no boundaries of nation or ethnicity or creed.

The good news proclaimed by Jesus is good news for you only insofar *as* it is also good news for your neighbor. This is not the way we generally imagine the good news. We want good news for ourselves, for my salvation, for my personal relationship with a Jesus Christ who died for *me*. In Christianity, such smallness of vision infects the Church down to the visceral core of its soul. "Abide with me," we sing.

Against the grain of such popular religiosity, Jesus read from the scroll of Isaiah the proclamation of good news for all those who suffer and are helpless and are outcast wherever they may be.

And then he preached his sermon: "Today this scripture has been fulfilled in your hearing."

At some considerable risk to his own safety, Jesus made it incandescently clear that the time of waiting for justice was over. In the way he lived and in the way he was teaching his people to live, this text was becoming visibly true at that very moment. Prophecy was being transformed into discipleship. The sermon was not so much interpretation as announcement. Hope was being transformed into action. This is what is going to get Jesus into trouble. It's what got King into trouble. It's the very heart of what it means to practice Christianity today: discipleship, proclamation, faith-filled action.

I eventually learned enough about the war in Vietnam that I added my voice to those who were so passionately protesting against it. Those of us who were university students were caught in an awkward position. We were, in the early years of the war, draft exempt. The sons of Appalachian coal miners and the sons of tobacco harvesters in Kentucky and inner-city African Americans were the ones fighting this war, in effect serving as point men for the rest of us. In the end, as much as I was opposed to this war, I decided out of a sense of solidarity with these young men that I had to enlist. Staying at university was just too much of a luxury. I signed up for Naval Officer's Candidate School and sailed through the exams, until it came to my eye test, and they discovered that I had this tendency to see double. They wouldn't take me. They wouldn't even draft me. "Why?" I asked. "You wouldn't know who to shoot, if you see double." "Shoot?" I said. "I don't want to shoot anyone. Why do you think I signed up for Naval Officer's Candidate School?"

I continued to protest the war, even more vigorously, aware of the inescapable ambiguity of what it means to live engaged with the world. As long as our holy texts are confined to Sunday morning readings rolled out in their three year lectionary cycle, innocuous, liturgical, finely spoken in the best plummy accent, they remain right where the powers and principalities want them to be. When they become the values that inform political and social action, it's not just unsettling for the authorities. Think of the disorientation in our ordinary Christian communities. Do our harvest festivals, bake sales and Wednesday night prayer meetings make this text clear as a living reality too? Is there any urgency about our Christian fellowship? Is there any risk?

Epiphany 4 C: "Thinking big"

Luke 4:21–30

Thinking like Jesus is thinking that is shaped by the future, in the way our celebration of the Lord's Supper, for instance, is an anticipation of what we call "the messianic banquet" in God's hoped-for kingdom. That fellowship, we imagine, will be one where "there is neither Jew nor Greek, neither bond nor free, neither male nor female," for we are all one in Christ Jesus (Galatians 3:28).

It is no act of religious imagination but statistical projection that in my home country, by the year 2040, the population will have no ethnic majority. Frank Yamada, in his inaugural address as the new president of my alma mater, McCormick Theological Seminary in Chicago, welcomed the prospect of such egalitarian democracy as good news. But, he said, "it doesn't mean racial inequality will vanish and racism will end, but that diversity will no longer be a goal or an ideal but a reality – a more diverse image of who we are as a people."

There is something alluring about trying to reduce life to the singular terms of a dominant majority. But, citing the Pentecost story in Acts, Yamada said, "God disrupts the one and creates many, cultures and languages, all in the plural. God prefers diversity over singularity."

Jesus is making a similar case against singularity in a sermon he gave in his hometown synagogue in Nazareth. Reading from Isaiah, he says, "The Spirit of the Lord is upon me, because he has anointed me to bring good news to the poor. He has sent me to proclaim release to the captives and recovery of sight to the blind, to let the oppressed go free, to proclaim the year of the Lord's favor."

His presentation was impressive. The elders in his hometown synagogue could hear every word he said. They were amazed at his polished public presence, his impressive pulpit manner. His sermon was mercifully short, and he had plenty of expression in his voice. But why was their village boy putting on such airs? Who did he think he was? As a member of a local village, you learn to keep your head down.

Jesus realizes straightaway that the message he is proclaiming from Isaiah is not going to be received here in Nazareth. It's not just that prophets aren't honored in their hometowns. It's the blinkered, narrow-minded village thinking by which we imagine ourselves as the focus of God's attention that is the problem. Actually, whole nations can fall into this kind of mind trap. "The failure of Western European civilization, indeed its hubris," Frank Yamada said in his inaugural address, "has been in its attempt to universalize human experience into its own culturally specific categories for understanding human life."

In this kind of thinking, the kind of people who are the focus of God's good news – the poor, the captives, the blind, the oppressed – are problems. For Jesus they represent an opportunity to be embraced, a new, broader form of community that has never before existed. And more, this opportunity was being embraced in this present moment. What Isaiah proclaimed is happening now as it is heard. As Paul had said, "now is the day of salvation" (2 Cor 6:2).

But not here in Nazareth. The elders of the Nazareth synagogue rise up in anger and drive him out of town. The lectionary implies that the Nazareth elders need to quit acting like children who thinks the world revolves around satisfying their own egocentric needs, and start acting like adults ("When I was a child, I spoke like a child, I thought like a child, I reasoned like a child; when I became an adult, I put an end to childish ways," 1 Corinthians 13.11).

We see here in the important position of the first episode of Jesus' ministry (in Luke's version of the story) a pattern we will see repeated throughout this Gospel and beyond, into Acts –

proclamation, rejection and moving on to marginalized communities who can hear, accept and celebrate the kind of transfiguration that enables them to live life as it had never been lived before, as neither Jew nor Greek, slave nor free, male nor female. This is the way it has always been. "They will fight against you," Jeremiah was told, "but they will not prevail" (Jeremiah 1.19).

Epiphany 5 C: "What we all preach"

Isaiah 6:1–8; Corinthians 15:1–11; Luke 5:1–11

Gary Skinner, Chicago Presbytery's executive presbyter in those days, stopped by my office at McCormick Theological Seminary one day with a list in his briefcase of current openings in the presbytery. Chicago Presbytery is the largest presbytery in the country, so this was an ample list. And it was depressing. Most of the list was so typically Presbyterian – middle class, suburban, huge congregations that had grown up on Norman Vincent Peale's *The Power of Positive Thinking*.

Finally, he got to the end of his list and said, "Here's one you won't be interested in." Two struggling city churches had banded together to scrape up enough money to offer an 80% call. The neighborhood was less than 1% English-speaking Protestant, but they sounded hungry, and ready to do something exciting. This captured my imagination. So I sent for their profile.

The profile said their ideal candidate would be an ordained, divorced woman with five or more years of experience in ministry. I had no experience in ministry. I felt defeated from the start. I wrote Skinner a note, asking if my lack of ordination would be a problem. He wrote back – the letter obviously dictated to his secretary – saying he didn't think my lack of *coordination* would be a problem. Little did he know.

Simon Peter, when he sees the magnificent catch of fish Jesus has orchestrated, falls down at the knees of Jesus, saying, "Go away from me, Lord, for I am a sinful man." Isaiah, meeting the majesty of God in the Temple, says, "Woe is me! I am lost, for I am a man of unclean lips, and I live among a people of unclean lips." Paul, describing his conversion experience's vision of Jesus, says, 1 Corinthians 15:8, "He was seen also by me," and the immediate effect was that all he previously might have boasted about became like rubbish (Philippians 3:8). The call to ministry has a way of diminishing us, convincing us of our inadequacies, before grace finally enables us to stand up and say, "Here I am. Send me." Grace accosts us. Joseph Ross, in a poem published in *Sojourners*, says of those hauling in the fish nets:

This time they
are the ones caught.

These call narratives are resurrection stories. The Gospel of John recognizes this by shifting Luke's great catch of fish story to a story about a call coming in a vision of the resurrected one (John 21:6–7). Paul says, regarding this call to ministry, "I have been crucified with Christ; and it is no longer I who live, but it is Christ who lives in me" (Galatians 2:19–20). The transformation is as profound as that. And Paul tells his people how he is in pain until "Christ is formed in you" (Galatians 4:19). They will live "no longer for themselves" (2 Corinthians 5:15). There is "no longer Jew or Greek, there is no longer slave or free, there is no longer male and female; for all of you are one in Christ Jesus" (Galatians 3:28). They will be changed, "in the twinkling of an eye" (1 Corinthians 15:52).

But change is not what people want. Herbert Marcuse describes the easy, uncritical and entrenched thinking of "one-dimensional man" as deriving its belief, norms and values from existing thought and social practice. Critical thought, on the other hand, seeks an alternative perspective from which to critique the way things are. It demands the courage to imagine the difference between fact and potential, appearance and reality.

I say the *courage* to imagine because the more conventional, uncritical, defensive modes of thinking and acting are so powerfully defended. Think of the massive expansion under Obama of the secret surveillance of US citizens by the National Security Agency and the crackdown on whistleblowers, as well as the assassinations of suspected terrorists by missiles fired by robot drones. In Israel, more security walls are being constructed as Netanyahu worries that refugees and African migrant workers are threatening the identity of the Jewish state. Here in Britain Theresa May raises the same tension as harsh new restrictions, reminiscent of Ezra 10:11, are laid on British people who have taken foreign spouses. This is what one-dimensional thinking can look like on a social and political level.

On a more psychological level, I am reminded of Ernest Becker's writing in *The Denial of Death*. Becker contends that a fear and denial of change lies behind our numerous "immortality projects", agendas that bring misery to our world in war, bigotry, genocide, racism, nationalism – as one group's hunger to be in control and without limit contends with another's.

Caroline Walker Bynum's *The Resurrection of the Body in Western Christianity, 200–1336*, shows how Christian tradition almost immediately departed from Paul's teaching on "change" to insist on resurrection as continuity, imagining physical continuity of bodily integrity after death and a world to come as a grander and more abundant version of this world. This is, essentially, where the Church remains today, with its one-dimensional theology of distorted hope.

Paul didn't have to convince the Corinthians about the resurrection. Paul speaks of the good news which the Corinthians received and in which they stand (1 Corinthians 15:1). What the Corinthians didn't understand was that resurrection was about change. The Corinthians thought the resurrection released them from all the requirements of the Law. All the laws and rules and regulations, for them, are kaput, done with, history. Grace is free. As a character in WH Auden's *For the Time Being* says, "I like committing crimes. God likes forgiving them. Really the world is admirably arranged."

Consequently, Paul had all kinds of problems with the Corinthian church – sexual immorality, pushing the poor aside as they grabbed after the best parts of the communion feast, bickering over who was making the best contribution to church life.

This is where the Corinthians are. So for all kinds of pastoral reasons this is where Paul starts. He starts right here, affirming their belief in the resurrection, and then moves them on from where they are to where they need to be. He moves them from a church with neither structure nor sense of fellowship to a critical understanding of a church that can be transformed into a community worthy of the name "body of Christ".

This is the good news I have always preached, Paul says, which you have heard and believed. This is the ground your faith stands on, the foundation of your salvation – that Christ died and rose again and was seen by Peter, then by all twelve apostles and once by over five hundred at once. No problem, the Corinthians are saying. This is, indeed, what they believe.

Then Paul says, "… and last of all, he was seen by me."

How was Paul a witness to the resurrection? Wasn't it at his conversion, on the road to Damascus? Wasn't it when Paul's life changed? His experience of the risen Christ was inseparable from the experience of his own re-birth, a change, a transformation from a zealous persecutor of the early church, an extremist (these are his own words) in defending his people's tradition. His call to apostleship marks a transition from this to a life shaped by love, a life empty of pride and full of compassion, free, self-critical and non-coercive. Christ, crucified, comes alive in Paul as the "Christ who lives in me" (Galatians 2:20).

By placing himself in this company of those who have been witnesses to the risen Christ, Paul implies that all who have gone before him have had this same experience, beginning with Peter. It is a mistake, by the way, for the NRSV to translate 1 Corinthians 15:5 as: "He appeared to Peter," when the verb here says: "He was seen by Peter," in the same way Paul says, in verse 8, "He was seen also by me" (*ōphthē ka'moi*) – a perceiver-grounded version of seeing more in keeping with Paul's expressed visionary experience of Jesus.

To see the risen Christ is to be called to discipleship. Thus Paul moves the Corinthians on from where they were to a new understanding, to where they had never asked or imagined themselves to be, as those liberated by Christ to live, now, *as* Christ, filled with all the fullness of God. Resurrection is inseparable from discipleship. "God, who... called me through his grace, was pleased to reveal his Son in me" (Galatians 1:15–16). Note that Paul didn't say his Son was revealed *to* me, but *in* me.

This change, from what Marcuse would call the mere acceptable appearance of what life is all about to the essence of what life *can be* all about, provokes the evidence in real life for the truth of resurrection. As soon as Paul concludes his discourse on resurrection here, he says, "Now concerning the collection for the saints..." (1 Corinthians 16:1). Here is life together as the living body of Christ in action. It's no "mystery". Or, if it is, like magicians Penn and Teller, Paul tells us how it's done. "Listen up! I will explain to you a mystery! We do not just fall asleep. We will all be changed" (1 Corinthians 15:51).

Epiphany 6 C: "The only earth we know"

Luke 6:17–26

The proximity of St. Valentine's Day always reminds me what a lonely place this earth is. Scientists, for instance, are in general agreement that there are other people out there – that, given the vast number of stars in our Milky Way galaxy, there are bound to be plenty of advanced civilizations out there somewhere. They can even pinpoint the most likely places in the galaxy to find them – far enough into the center to have all the right bits to make a habitable planet, but yet far enough out to avoid being bumped or scorched or frazzled by neighbors.

But it is next to impossible to make connections.

Astrophysicist Rasmus Björk says we could send eight probes out into the galaxy, each one travelling ten times the speed of NASA's current probe making its way to Saturn, and each of these eight probes could send out eight mini-probes, so that there are these eight probes and these sixty four mini-probes from this lonely planet searching through the most likely territory for a suitable companion.

But it would take ten billion years to cover just 4% of the galaxy.

That's how far apart we are. Even if we were able to home in on the stray signals of some extraterrestrial radio or television broadcast, say an extraterrestrial version of *Blind Date*, it would still take a million years to make the connection. Our planet is indeed a lonely planet. This is the cosmological version of what Elizabeth Hardwick, in *Sleepless Nights*, describes as "missing the eye of the needle trying to thread your way through love."

It's bad enough trying to find other people here on earth, separated as we are not so much by miles as by fear and duplicity and insecurity and the need to protect ourselves. People prefer to live alone, says Eric Klinenberg in *Going Solo: The Extraordinary*

Rise and Surprising Appeal of Living Alone. The New York University sociologist studied single living in America, where 50% of adults are single, but in Britain, Scandinavia and Japan the figures are even higher.

We might be tempted to rail against the narcissism of contemporary life. Klinenberg sees the upsurge in single living as symptomatic of a society's growing wealth, like owning cars or eating meat. But others, like Richard Sennett in *The Fall of Public Man*, might say that this upsurge in single living has to do with the inappropriate and unsustainable emphasis that, since Victorian times, has been given to family life and interpersonal intimacy at the expense of public life. The people Klinenberg interviewed were not anxious and desperate but, by and large, convinced that they had the best deal. Sennett describes the distortion of human relationships in unrealistic warmth and closeness as dangerous. Apparently some people are beginning to realize this.

Luke, in what we call the "Sermon on the Plain", changes Matthew's "blessed are the poor in spirit" to just plain "blessed are the poor". Luke puts Matthew's famous "Sermon on the Mount" down here on the plain, on the level of the people, where the grace of God finds its proper grounding in public responsibility. The intimacy of what the Religious Right calls "Family Values" can deflect our discipleship from its proper focus on public justice. "Blessed is the womb that bore you and the breasts that nourished you," shouts a woman in the crowd. But Jesus says, "Blessed rather are those who hear the word of God and obey it" (Luke 11:27–28).

Dietrich Bonhoeffer, in *Life Together*, said what the Church too often promotes is this warm, cozy cure for existential loneliness – the bonding with like-minded people, familiar liturgies, blessed assurances the Church Growth Movement speaks of as keys to success. But such an inward-looking focus is, again, dangerous. What life together really needs to be about is a more public engagement with the real world as neighbors. That is the more appropriate message for St. Valentine's Day.

Discovering how we are to live doesn't come easy for Christians.

In February 1977, Oscar Romero was named Archbishop of San Salvador, a conservative, pietistic, committed to defeating the radical political agendas of his left-leaning priests. But little by little the experience of ministering among poor people tightly gripped in the clutches of the wealthy changed his heart, until he could proclaim, publicly:

> I am a shepherd who, with his people, has begun to learn a beautiful and difficult truth: our Christian faith requires that we submit ourselves to this world. The world that the Church must serve is the world of the poor, and the poor are the ones who decide what it means for the Church to really live in the world.

The poor can show the Church how to get real, to live in the world with integrity. Matthew has "blessed are those who hunger for righteousness." Luke, bluntly, has "blessed are the hungry."

One of my first experiences in ministry included the task of forming an evangelism committee to help build up the membership. It didn't work, so I dropped it like the proverbial hot potato. Instead, I gathered the rather large group of singles in the church – young adults, older people who had never married or were divorced – to meet socially and for informal worship. Social ministries like volunteering at soup kitchens and organizing a clothing pantry grew out of this group, and it began to flourish. Klinenberg, whose research I didn't know at the time, gives us a hint on why this kind of strategy clicks with singles. Community, public life is still important for them. What is needed are links between solitary and communal experiences. It seems to me that this is almost a definition of what we mean by 'church'. But it's more than church. Leonie Sandercock, in *Towards Cosmopolis*, speaks of city planning in the same spirit, inspired by postmodern, post-colonial and feminist critique – creating new kinds of public space that celebrate community and diversity.

It is not easy for the church to be such a matchmaker. There is massive institutional resistance. It is as if the Church is like this small ball of earth spinning in its splendid isolation in the vast, black emptiness of space. Alone on St. Valentine's Day.

If this life lived in cozy, interpersonal, family intimacy is the only life we hope for, Paul says in 1 Corinthians 15:19, then of all people we are the most to be pitied. Christian hope is for something more, a life engaged in the healing of a broken world: life together.

Transfiguration C: "On the road with Jesus"

Luke 9:28–36

This extraordinary tale of the Transfiguration is one of those stories conveying an experience too big for ordinary words. The story begins with Jesus going up a mountain to pray. Jesus brings Peter and James and John with him, and as he is praying they have this vision of him transformed in appearance, whiter than white, transfigured, and then they see Moses and Elijah standing beside him.

Thus far, Luke's Transfiguration story is straight out of the Gospel of Mark. But then Luke adds something of his own. He has Peter and the others hear Moses and Elijah speaking of the departure which Jesus was about to accomplish in Jerusalem.

What do they mean by his "departure"? Are they speaking about his death? The word 'departure' is our translation of Luke's Greek. The Greek word here is 'exodus'. What does the word 'exodus' bring to mind? The second book of the Bible? The whole story of the departure of the Hebrew people from their slavery in Egypt?

At Passover our Jewish brothers and sisters eat unleavened bread – what they call the "bread of affliction" – as a way of remembering how they came out of Egypt in great haste, with no time to bake proper loaves of bread. They do this to remember the day of their departure, the day of their exodus. This is a loaded word, isn't it? Profoundly so. It reaches into the depths of what it means to be the people of God.

And by this simple word 'exodus' Luke ties the Transfiguration story to the larger pilgrimage we make from Bethlehem to Jerusalem and on, in the Book of Acts, to Rome. In Exodus, God says to Moses, "I have seen the misery of my people in Egypt; I have heard their cry… and I have come down to deliver them from the Egyptians, and to bring them up out of that land to a good and broad land." And Mary, in the Magnificat, sings that God "has looked with favor on the lowliness of his servant." Luke's Jesus speaks of real material poverty in his sermon on the plain, not just spiritual poverty, because the kingdom proclaimed will bring an end to the economics of exploitation. In his inaugural sermon he proclaims good news to the poor, the captive, the oppressed, and in Luke 7:22 Jesus tells the disciples of John the Baptist to go tell John that people can see this is already happening. In the Parable of the Great Supper, Luke's addition to the version he got from Matthew has it that the servants are ordered to bring in "the poor, the maligned, the blind and the lame." Zacchaeus, so delighted that Jesus is coming to his house for tea, vows to share half his wealth with the poor. These are exodus stories of God's preferential option for the poor. And then there is the crowning story of all, the story of the passion and execution, in which solidarity with the poor becomes complete. "Today you will be with me in Paradise," Jesus says to the condemned man at his side.

Acts then unfolds the implications of such solidarity in terms of the growth of a new community. This too is the exodus story: "All who believed were together and had all things in common; they would sell their possessions and goods and distribute the proceeds to all, as any had need," Acts 2:44–45.

Immediately after this Transfiguration vision Jesus "set his face toward Jerusalem." The Mount of Transfiguration becomes a vantage point looking ahead into the journey toward exodus. In the season of Lent, Transfiguration Sunday stands at a precipice overlooking a journey toward that climactic act of solidarity on Good Friday that will also be our journey.

Can you count the times when you have had to set your face toward Jerusalem, whatever that may have been for you, in a resolve to face a difficult situation that, for your own integrity and for the well-being of your world, could not be put off? The journey is not just something Jesus did. The journey you take transfigures the way you see the world, and transfigures the world. In Birmingham, Alabama, in Belfast, in Syria, in Jerusalem, defeated integrity always outshines a triumphant evil.

Sadly, and too often, the Church can stand in the way of taking this world-transforming exodus journey. The Welsh poet RS Thomas wrote:

> ... History shows us
> he was too big to be nailed to the wall
> of a stone chapel, yet still we crammed him
> between the boards of a black book.

We need Christians who are poets and artists who can look at the ordinary and see there something magnificent and miraculous, as on the Mount of Transfiguration, something that allows words and images to become liberated from the confining boards of a black book and allow exodus to happen.

Ash Wednesday C: "Resurrection's preview"

2 Corinthians 5:20b–6:10; Matthew 6:1–6, 16–21

Just before the beginning of our text from 2 Corinthians, Paul says, "If anyone is in Christ, there is a new creation: everything old has passed away; see, everything has become new" (2 Corinthians 5:17). This new creation has been made possible through God's reconciling work in Christ. "In Christ God was reconciling the world to himself" (2 Corinthians 5:19), Paul says. And he goes on. God is in us now, reconciling the world to himself. We are called to be ambassadors of reconciliation, God's teammates. We're working together.

This is very affirmative stuff – not the stuff I expected to see on Ash Wednesday. And there is more. This is not something we have to wait for. It's happening now. "Now is the day of salvation," Paul says (2 Corinthians 6:2). Who needs Easter?

In Wales the word 'now' means some time in the indefinite future. When dinner is on the table and you call your daughter to come downstairs to join the rest of the family, she says, "I'm coming now," meaning in about five or ten minutes. If your kitchen is ankle deep from a broken water pipe and you call the plumber, he says, "I'll be there now in a minute," meaning maybe in half an hour if you are lucky. In Wales *Apocalypse Now* is *Apocalypse Now in a Minute.*

But here, with Paul, the day of salvation is really now – the immediate, contemporaneous moment. It's like having Easter without having to wade through Lent.

This is the way Lent happens in Wales. It seems to start as well as end with Easter. So I found my first Lent in Wales to be a very disorienting experience indeed.

I had always seen Lent as a penitential season, beginning on Ash Wednesday with wearing the ashes of our mortality. Such a reading of Lent was not part of my American Presbyterian tradition, but I was working in an ecumenical environment. The church I had been serving in Chicago had started out Evangelical and Reformed, which was itself a union between German Lutherans and Calvinists. There was a large book of services from the E & Rs in the church office, bound in red leather. I could see that their liturgical heritage was much higher than what I had grown up with. And besides, many of the relatives of church members seemed to be Lutheran. There were always friendly quibbles between the Swedes and the Norwegians in the congregation about how to serve coffee – how close to the rim you filled the cup, how much milk. You didn't dare serve it Norwegian style to a Swede.

When the Evangelical and Reformed denomination and the Congregationalists united in 1957, St. James became part of the United Church of Christ. Then they took in a small band of Presbyterians whose church had closed, and they became St. James United Church. When they found out they were obligated to be sending financial contributions to both the UCC and the Presbyterians, they decided to just be Presbyterian, the cheaper option. But they still remained Evangelical and Reformed in spirit, and on the high church Lutheran side of that original union.

So going with the people where they were and departing from my Presbyterian roots, I learned to preside at an Ash Wednesday service, complete with ashes. I fit in.

But that kind of high liturgy would never wash in the United Reformed Church community I was serving on a sprawling Welsh council estate on the west side of Cardiff.

In the first place, the heritage of the United Reformed Church in Wales was pure Congregationalist, undiluted by ecumenical entanglements. They seemed to have taken to the advice from Matthew in our Ash Wednesday reading: "Whenever you fast, do not look dismal, like the hypocrites." They couldn't get their heads around the Anglican idea of an "outward and visible sign of an inward and spiritual grace. " Any sense of outward sign was hypocritical.

Secondly, and more significantly, Wales in general just doesn't do Lent very well, for deep-seated cultural reasons. The biggest festival of the year for all denominations and Christians and non-Christians alike is St. David's Day, the first of March. St. David's Day easily trumps Ash Wednesday. I remember my first Lent here. A strong, warm, wet wind swept through the streets of the council estate on Ash Wednesday. White clouds marched bravely across an intensely blue sky. Lawns and every bit of green were covered in festal daffodils, the national flower of Wales. The fecundity seemed more like Easter than Ash Wednesday. St. David's Day was a day for celebration. The children were dressed in traditional Welsh costume, with aprons and bonnets and lace shawls and gingham skirts. We gathered in the church hall that evening to sing songs in Welsh, read poetry and feast on the traditional lamb stew, '*cawl*'. There was no way I was going to intrude on all this festivity with my pot of ashes. It seemed as if everyone had read, and believed, what Paul says: "Now is the day of salvation!" No need to wait for Easter.

I had thought it would be different. So many of the Welsh hymn tunes, like Aberystwyth or Ebenezer, are in mournful minor keys. Many in Wales remain conscious of loss of independence, as people had in the American South after the Civil War or in Japan after WWII. The Prince of Wales is the son of the English monarch. And Welsh life is hard, particularly in the mining valleys where memories of the ever-present danger of death still linger. And it was hard on the council estate where I was serving. We had all the worst statistics for things like alcoholism, mental illness, family breakup, school drop-outs, learning disabilities, drugs and general poverty. Loan sharks preyed from house to house on people's desperation.

So where was the mourning? Where did the readiness for

festivity come from? Paul says, 2 Corinthians 5:21, Christ "was made to be sin who knew no sin." Christ entered into a no-holding-back solidarity with the rejected, the defeated and the maligned. This is what it means to 'be' sin, yet know no sin. It is the trajectory of a believer's life as we see it mandated in Philippians 2, where we are asked to "have the same mind as Christ," who emptied himself, taking the form of a servant, not as a feature of defeat but as the glad victory of a compassionate life in the face of all that threatens it. Here, I suggest, is the spirit of the 1984 Miners' Strike and the chapel socialism of the Welsh valleys. And it is not just the political spirit of Wales, but the spirit that gathered its churches and chapels to ecumenical *Gymanfa Ganu* nights of community hymn-singing and still brings singers and poets to gather for the annual Eisteddfod festival.

Ministers who go off on their sabbaticals to study Celtic spirituality will tell you that Latin penitential practices never quite caught on in Wales. The Celtic spirituality of Wales was much more earthy, tied to landscape and weather and life-affirming. Resurrection was about the victory of love over the omnipresent experience of death and sorrow.

Of course the people in their congregations don't know all this deep heritage stuff. But the spirit is still there, unnamed but lived. I had to learn a new way of being Christian. I can hear them saying what Paul says in our Ash Wednesday reading from 2 Corinthians 6: "We are treated... as sorrowful, yet always rejoicing; as poor, yet making many rich; as having nothing, and yet possessing everything."

Lent 1 C: "Tempted as we are"

Luke 4:1–13

When in my youth I had a summer job teaching children to swim, my first task was to help them experience being in the water without fear. So the first thing I did was to teach them how to float. In order to float, you simply have to learn to let go. Lean back in the water and allow it to carry you – there is a bit of a trick in how you arch your back, but I never met a child who couldn't float. The trick is to let go, but the temptation is to fight, because you want to be in control. If this remains your agenda, if you fear the water, you will never learn the art of swimming.

The temptation to fight the water, to be in control, is the same temptation as the first temptation, the temptation faced by our first parents, in the Garden of Eden, when the serpent said: "You will not die. You will be like gods." The temptation is to grab at life like a possession, to believe that you can control it, so that you never have to die, you never have to fall in love, you never have to learn anything or understand anything that refuses to conform to the tidy little world of self-reference.

So the temptation Jesus experienced out here in the wilderness is the temptation we all face every day, the temptation to force life to conform to our control. "In most of my life I want and demand a great deal of control," writes Daniel Callahan in *The Troubled Dream of Life: In Search of a Peaceful Death*. "But I came to notice that… my desire for maximum control has not always served me well. It did not create a person I could invariably admire."

The first temptation is to turn stones into bread, an act of magic that like all acts of magic would have the universe conform to our wishes immediately, without waiting. The Japanese theologian Koyama says that a nuclear weapon is magic in this sense: we are tempted to use them because they get instant results without having to work through all the bother of negotiation and compromise and all the tiresome requirements of our ordinary humanity. Violence is always a kind of magic; whether domestic or in international affairs, violence is resorted to in order to force conformity to one's own will without having to bother with the requirements of relationships.

Magic implies that the real world doesn't really exist, or isn't acknowledged to exist. We wall ourselves off from the real world as if we were living in one of those walled-off, security-guarded suburbs they have in my home country, never having to deal with people who are unlike ourselves. I once visited a professor at Ben-Gurion University who lived in a suburban Jewish community near Be'er Sheva, fenced off with locked gates against its Bedouin neighbors. It was a soul-chilling experience.

There was a survey published recently on the state of religion in ten countries across the world – Britain, India, the States, South Korea and so on. Britain scored higher than any on xenophobia, blaming our problems on people of other faiths, a stance that is not just statistical. The British National Party has made its presence known here in Cardiff demonstrating against the presence of refugees.

Britain also scored a distinctive discomfort with suffering. Coddled, affluent Britain found suffering a prime reason for not believing in God, whereas in a country like India where raw human need is a daily reality, suffering presented no barrier to belief. These are the kinds of statistical scores a society gets that has given in to the temptation of magic, whose reality becomes the glittering chrome and glass facades of our giant shopping centers and the xenophobic fears of the *Daily Express*.

So, we see that Jesus is tempted in every way as we are to make the world conform to his desires. But he doesn't give in.

In the second temptation Jesus imagines himself controlling all the kingdoms of the world. He would be a superhuman Messiah, meeting no resistance as he worked for good. He would have no need for courage, therefore, and would experience no fear. He would be invulnerable. He would exercise ultimate power, if only he would bow down, as so many do, to worship that spiritual impulse we all have for such invincibility.

But this isn't what worship means. Or at least this isn't what worshipping God means. To worship God is to become vulnerable to what is ever beyond us and un-nameable. In worshipping God we become companions of the intimate dreams of others and are enabled to accompany the hopes of the brokenhearted. What Jesus is tempted to now is a world of power centered on himself. As St. Augustine described sin as an incurvature of the spirit in upon itself, so Jesus is tempted by a vision of vocation that turns inward. He is tempted in every way as we are, but he does not give in.

The third temptation is the temptation of fundamentalism, the temptation to reduce the rhapsodic passion of Psalm 91 to the small literal meaning of its words, as if a company of angels would literally hold us up, lest we stub a foot against a stone – a lovely thought, meant to convey the security with God we find when we take on responsibility for one another as faithful members of this covenant community, but why would anyone take it literally?

Fundamentalism is the curse of all religion anywhere, as religious institutions in the interest of orthodoxy collapse poetic transcendence into the small world of dogma and rigid fact (this happens in politics and among non-believers as well). Again, the temptation is an incurvature of the spirit inward, a nervous defense of the most impoverished rigidity of language, so stripped of its vitality that it is of no more use to our hungry hearts than the record of a warehouse inventory.

There is an added factor here. Language that turns in upon itself like this becomes, again, a tool for those who seek to control. It forms part of a defense mechanism, a stony fortress built in fear of others. Fundamentalism invariably gets linked with intolerance, xenophobic political agendas and violence. In this temptation we reduce the breadth of our world to what can be pointed to, controlled, and purchased like pornography, pointing to what is merely visible, not nuanced with the richness of human ambiguity, but made into an object impervious to challenge, privileged, dominating.

Jesus was tempted in every way as we are to reduce language to its literal, legalistic, fundamental and inert level of meaning. Again, the temptation was to turn defensively in upon himself. He knew the answer had to do with where he chose to stand, and with whom he chose to take a stand, in order to redeem the imaginative possibilities of a kingdom where good news is preached to the poor. He did not give in. In the end, he found his proper place between two thieves, and found the kingdom he proclaimed hidden where Satan cannot see it, in the cross.

Lent 2 C: "Gimme Shelter"

Luke 13:31–35

The image of Jesus as a mother hen sheltering her chicks under her wings is a marvelous, marvelous image of security. The people of Jerusalem are crying, as in the Rolling Stones song, "If I don't get some shelter… I'm gonna fade away." Jesus wants to hold them in his arms, protecting them.

Think about this image, think about it emotionally, and you begin to understand something central to the Gospel of Luke. This Gospel celebrates the faces in the crowd, little people like Zacchaeus who climb trees for a better look and humble shepherds who hurry down to Bethlehem, tearaways like the Prodigal Son, crowds of people like the growing community of women, the multitude of disciples shouting after Jesus as he rides into Jerusalem, the uncountable number of people looking in from the edges who find inclusion, affirmation, celebration. The Gospel of Luke is like a kaleidoscope of the unwanted who find themselves, suddenly, made special and central. They become a community, a fellowship that itself becomes a healing fellowship, continuing the ministry of Jesus after his execution with a revolutionary inclusivity, embracing the discarded in Christ's name. They become the body of Christ, the literal bodily presence of Christ alive in the world.

All this is summed up in the desire of Jesus to embrace the people of Jerusalem. That is the beauty of this story. You can see this kind of beauty living in churches all over the world. I was speaking the other day, for instance, to a young woman, a friend of a friend from years ago, who serves as a minister for a church in Botswana. She describes her church as a place of refuge, a human community in a place of desperation, with the highest HIV/AIDS infection rate in the world, with poverty like we can barely imagine, with a deep hunger for God. And the church, she says, finds its life in an intimate, caring, responsive fellowship that is like a large, supportive family in a world where families are being torn apart.

So there is this beautiful possibility of creating new communities hidden in this story, communities that will be as numerous as the descendants of Abraham, like the stars of the night sky.

But there is also tension in this story, deep tension. Herod, whom Jesus calls "that fox", is no mother hen. He is out to get Jesus, and Jerusalem itself seems to conspire against Jesus' efforts to build an inclusive, caring community. Jerusalem is the place where they kill prophets. A friend of mine, one of our synod moderators in the United Reformed Church, says church leaders kill prophets. They are too committed to protecting the status quo to risk innovation. The powers-that-be look after the security of the structures they manage, thus making the world very insecure for flesh-and-blood people who have to live in those structures.

Cities like Jerusalem can be places of profound insecurity. At City United Reformed Church we used Philip Jenkins' book, *The Next Christendom: The Coming of Global Christianity*, for a Lent study one year. We read of the new mega-cities of the southern hemisphere in which Christian communities are struggling to embrace those who have come into the city from rural areas lost, confused and easily exploited in a dog-eat-dog urban jungle.

Fifty years ago, for instance, the Nigerian city of Lagos was a ramshackle port community roughly the size of Cardiff. Fifteen years ago Lagos numbered 1.3 million. Today, with a population density of 20,000 people per square kilometer, Lagos is almost ten times as densely populated as Rotterdam.

People get lost in places like Lagos, and in other fast-growing mega-cities like Lima, São Paulo, Karachi or Bombay. Cities like Lagos suffer desperately from congestion and pollution and lack of public services. Lagos is deeply divided with tension between Christians and Muslims. Fraud is rampant as people struggle to survive. They are desperate. They hunger for the kind of security

Jesus would like to provide for the people of Jerusalem. "Jerusalem, Jerusalem," he cries out, verse 34: "How often have I desired to gather your children together as a hen gathers her brood under her wings!"

You can imagine how an impoverished people respond. Lagos has been the scene of some of the biggest evangelistic rallies in world history. In 1998 a revival gathered a congregation of close to two million. In 2000, comparable numbers responded to German Pentecostal evangelist Reinhard Bonnke's invitation to "Come and receive your miracle". Religion becomes a desperate search for a heavenly insurance policy in an insecure world.

What is security? My son once had a job as a security guard. He has a phenomenal memory, and within the first hour on the job had this huge complicated set of keys memorized. Security, popularly conceived, is about locks and keys. It's about high walls between Jewish and Palestinian communities in Israel. It's about cluster bombs and Trident missiles and pre-emptive strikes. It's about controlling world oil resources and getting rich.

Christian security, though, looks very different. Christian security takes that journey with Jesus to Jerusalem, to the place where they kill prophets but where you know you have to be, if you are going to be true to yourself, true to your God and true therefore to your neighbor. Jesus' journey to Jerusalem will not be stopped or diminished by the threats of those who control the security of our institutions.

For Jesus, embracing his neighbors was risky business, but it was a lover's embrace, entering into the fullness of a shared reality as lovers do when they take on one another's spirit, mind and flesh. Entering into the unmediated reality of the world like this is like the kind of journey through the desert described by Presbyterian theologian Belden Lane in a book called *The Solace of Fierce Landscapes: Exploring Desert and Mountain Spirituality*. The journey is a spiritual journey that is, Lane says, "risky in the best sense of the term." Here he confronted the raw personal experiences of the slow, painful death of his mother and, decades earlier, the suicide of his father, death and loss stripped of all the denials and illusions we normally use to hide under. Taking such a spiritual journey, he says, "You travel into terrain that you most want to avoid, that you want to forget about. You go there and you don't run away and you work through it, and then you have the experience of Isaiah 35," the desert coming into bloom as Isaiah proclaimed it would for exiles coming back home to Jerusalem.

"My fear," writes Lane, "is that much of what we call 'spirituality' today is overly sanitized and sterile, far removed from the anguish of pain, the anchoredness of real places." Without the tough-minded discipline of what Lane calls the desert-mountain experience, spirituality loses its demand for justice, takes no risks and becomes mired in a swamp of mere self-realization. Christian spirituality demands a tough-minded discipline of living unprotected in the world alongside our most vulnerable neighbors, in all its honest suffering. This is what we seek when in the song we ask our God to guide us as pilgrims through this "barren land".

While ordinary security is a withdrawal behind protective walls, checkpoints and hardened missile silos, Christians find their security in being true to their faith no matter what the consequences. Anyone telling you that the Christian life can be found without risk and shared brokenness is trying to sell you something.

Lent 3 C: "Just desserts?"

Luke 13:1–9

They still had freak shows at the Hancock County agricultural fair back in the 1950s. The annual summer visit of a community of bearded ladies, enormously fat men, dwarfs and people with reptilian skin reminded those of us who never wandered far from our small town how beautiful we were.

The scandals that pass for news in the tabloid press remind people how virtuous they are. With the Leveson Inquiry on press standards there is a lot of talk about how important the tabloids are in exposing corruption. Too often they seem like a print version of a freak show.

The BBC is supposed to be above all this, but even the knife in the back betrayals and the murders reported on the News at Ten have their appeal in reminding us how blameless we are. As we look at all the trouble people get into we sit back to congratulate ourselves on how truly fortunate we are.

We are lucky, we say. And while luck may seem to some to carry with it a kind of moral superiority, in reality being lucky is simply being in a different kind of accident.

In the Gospel story for this Sunday of Lent we overhear the kind of gossip people indulge in in order to feel better about themselves: Hey! Did you hear that Pilate killed a bunch of Galileans? Did you hear how he mixed their blood with the blood of their sacrifices? How gross! I'm so glad that didn't happen to me! In the absence of a tabloid press such a gruesome rumor had to be carried by word of mouth.

How awful! He mixed their blood with the blood of sacrificed animals. How awful! What could they have done to deserve it?

Jesus turns on them. You think they were worse sinners than you? And those eighteen guys who got killed by the tower that collapsed at Siloam? Do you think they were worse sinners than you?

I tell you one thing, Jesus says. If you don't straighten out and start flying right, the same thing or worse will happen to you.

Sometimes the word of our Lord is a rhetorical threat, like when I was pulling faces as a kid and my mother would warn me that if I didn't stop it my face would stay that way. It is a mistake to take what Jesus is saying literally, as if Pilate would really get them, too, if they didn't repent, or get you, for that matter. It is a mistake to think that we are speaking here of the mechanics of divine justice, as if towers would start falling on us if we did not learn to behave. This is not the way God operates.

Part of growing up is to realize that lots of things happen to people simply because things happen. Think of how terrible it would be to live in a world where towers did fall on sinners.

Some people don't happen to be standing under towers when they fall. Other people do.

Some people happen to be born in the slums of São Paulo. Others happen to be born in Chipping Norton. This is not because we are good people or bad people. It is because different accidents happen to different people.

If the only reason for behaving were to keep towers from falling on our heads, the only basis for moral action would be to save our own skin, and that is just not a very adult sense of what it means to live responsibly.

Jesus pushes us to think in a deeper way. Like the gardener who is patient with the fig tree that does not bear fruit, who prunes it, digs manure around its roots, cares for it, Jesus teaches us to take responsibility for the world around us. Jesus nurtures us and encourages our faith to mature, that we might build up those who now scandalize us, so that they become like the well-tended fig tree, and one day flourish.

We are responsible for a world that is not our fault. This is what it means to live as Jesus lived – taking on the concerns of neighbors.

What is fair and not fair has nothing to do with it. The grace of God is not fair. It is the sheer gift of love, coming as free as the rain, and teaching us to be just as gracious to others. Be compassionate as your father in heaven is compassionate, Jesus says in another place, Luke 6:36. Learn to give a damn. At the end of the day there is only one kind of fair in this world, and that is the county agricultural fair.

But what if someone really does screw up? What if it genuinely is their fault? Shouldn't they be taken out and given a good spanking?

Jesus seems to imply that the motivation for doing so is only to satisfy our own need for moral superiority, the kind of smug self-satisfaction we get by visiting a freak show or reading the tabloids.

People need the freedom to screw up in order to learn. Screwing up is a necessary experience in a life that makes any significant moral progress. Give the fig tree another chance, Jesus says. Seventy times seven extra chances, he says in another place.

Our job as Christians is not to condemn, but to nurture, to apply the manure of resourcing and encouragement and affirmation to the roots of our growing humanity. God knows, we grow by our mistakes and our scars and we thrive by grace, and we are called to be gracious to one another.

Is it all just desserts, then? Is the Christian life all pudding and cake? Of course not. This is no wishy-washy liberalism here. This is the nature of rigorous moral engagement with neighbors from a Christian point of view, and it can get you crucified. It is not the easy way. It is against the grain. It is not a business for wimps who need their fragile egos affirmed by reading the scandal sheets and visiting freak shows.

Lent 4 C: "Home"

Luke 15:1–3, 11b–32

The cover of a recent issue of *Heritage in Wales* magazine features a classic example of Welsh Revival architecture and an intriguing question: "Salvation for Welsh Chapels?" The expert from the Welsh Religious Buildings Trust says chapels have been closing for years. That is no big news. But we are now approaching a tipping point, he says. The collapse of the Welsh Revival chapel culture is going to be facing an even steeper decline in the near future.

It is interesting that the article describes the preservation of these dysfunctional relics as their "salvation", as if the word salvation meant a kind of preservation in formaldehyde of a culture that has resolutely refused to move into the exciting, dynamic world of God's always-emerging kingdom.

It's not just the Welsh Religious Buildings Trust or CADW or the practice of slapping listed building status on our Victorian heritage that is essentially blasphemous in its understanding of what church is all about. At its heart, the Church itself is guilty of such blasphemy as it slaps preservation orders on the creeds, liturgical practices, the gender bias and the clerical dress of a long departed age.

The familiar sin-repentance-forgiveness sequence is one of the primary mechanisms by which a conservative society maintains its authority. Indeed, this story of the Prodigal Son was used by schoolmasters in late sixteenth century Britain as a means of reinforcing the example of contrition and obedience to a fatherly authority. "Father," the returned Prodigal says, in a well-rehearsed speech reminiscent of the Prayer Book's prayer of humble access, "I have sinned against God and against you; I am no longer worthy to be called your son."

The schoolmasters would have their pupils act out the story

dramatically to drive in its moral in a play that became the most popular schoolboy drama of its day. Thomas Nashe's character Jack Wilton, in *The Unfortunate Traveller* (1594), described it as being "so filthily acted, so leathernly set forth, as would have moved laugher in Heraclitus."

It was popular with the schoolmasters because they thought the disastrous consequences of youthful folly it dramatizes would teach pupils a valuable moral lesson.

On the other hand, it was popular with the pupils themselves because it was so much fun to play the wastrel and his friends in their debauchery, debauchery that increasingly dominated the play as it grew in popularity until it got out of hand and the whole thing was scrapped from the curriculum.

Curiously, neither reason for the play's popularity focused on what is central to the story. Its proper focus is on the prodigality of the father, his unsparing excess, his reckless extravagance in celebrating the return of the ne'er-do-well younger son. He was lost, but now is found. He was dead, but now is alive. This is the joy of resurrection.

The original readership for the Gospel of Luke was the new community of Gentile Christians. What they would have seen here was the often heated conflict between the original Jewish followers of Jesus and these newly arrived Gentiles. For them the story of the Prodigal would have been the story they were experiencing, the story of the original followers of Jesus grousing about the welcome given to all these newcomer ne'er-do-wells.

The original Jewish followers of Jesus would have thought belonging to "the Way", as the Jesus movement was called, included keeping faith with classic Judaism, Jewish dietary laws, circumcision, the whole ball of wax. The late-arriving Gentiles, the readership to whom this Gospel is largely pitched, brought a breath of fresh air, an eager faith that transformed the hearts and minds of Jew and Gentile alike, broke down walls that stood between them, and allowed Paul to say what had never in human history been said before:

> There is no longer Jew or Greek, there is no longer slave or free, there is no longer male and female, for all of you are one in Christ Jesus.
> – Galatians 3:28

Far from a story reinforcing the values of a conservative society, this is a story about a profound cultural shift, the painful transition the loyal, never-wavering faithful had to make and the affirmation of this influx of new arrivals with different ways of doing things.

What happens to a society that refuses to budge? Jared Diamond has studied the society of Norwegian settlers in Greenland, for instance, that stubbornly kept trying to live as Europeans when it was wholly inappropriate and self-destructive to do so. In *Collapse: How Societies Choose to Fail or Survive*, Diamond describes how they imported luxury European household goods. Their clergy imported vestments and jewels and sent their linen ruff collars back to Norway to be starched and pressed. They imported bells and stained glass for their churches, and in order to pay for all this they devoted critical resources to exporting luxury goods back to Europe like ivory and polar bear hides. They never learned to fish. Their sheep overgrazed the vulnerable Greenland landscape. In the end they all starved to death.

Too many of our churches find their security in the same way the Welsh Religious Trust conceives of salvation – preserving the past. In Scripture salvation does not preserve. Salvation transforms, from brokenness to wholeness, from captivity to liberation, oppression to dignity, death to life. We shall be changed, Paul says, "in the twinkling of an eye." Think of what it would mean for our woodworm-ridden, antiquated Welsh chapels to have CADW slap a *salvation* order on them that required a renewal and revitalization that might even require demolition of what is in order to build something new more fitting for the twenty-first century: new wineskins for new wine.

I remain confident that there are churches that can be sufficiently far-sighted and selfless and deep thinking enough to experience a fellowship that is not only a fellowship with one another but a fellowship with God, a fellowship therefore that takes risks, and makes the hard and unpopular choices that will enable a generation yet unborn, and one very, very different from ourselves to praise the name of the Lord. When that happens, we will truly have come home to the Father.

Lent 5 C: "Simple gifts"

John 12:1–8

A friend from seminary days spent her internship year on a remote Alaskan island, where it was the duty of the minister to prepare bodies for burial, washing them, sealing body cavities, shrouding them. Mary washes the feet of Jesus with pure nard and then wipes them with her hair for a towel. This is an exquisitely intimate act.

Where else in the Gospel of John do we hear of washing feet? Of course. It is in John's version of the Last Supper. Here, instead of the familiar words spoken over the bread and wine, we have Jesus with bowl and towel washing his disciples' feet, as a way of teaching the deep, life-giving sense of hospitality that the bread and the wine are meant to convey. "If I, your Lord and Teacher," Jesus says, verse 14, "if I have washed your feet, you also ought to wash one another's feet." "By this everyone will know that you are my disciples," he says later, verse 35, "if you have love for one another."

So you see what is happening here? Mary is anticipating this Gospel of love that lies at the heart of John's Gospel. Unlike the male disciples, she does not have to be taught. It is a spontaneous gesture, a lavish demonstration of love that the disciples have such difficulty comprehending.

Judas, who serves as treasurer for the disciples, objects to this waste of money. The ointment could be sold and the money given to the poor, he says. Our narrator explains that he has no concern for the poor, as he pretends. His motive for keeping the money in the common purse is greed, selfish, self-absorbed, self-protecting greed, the polar opposite of the foot-washing compassion Mary demonstrates and Jesus tries to teach his disciples.

Jesus, in a sop to placate Judas' professed concern for the poor, says: "The poor will always be with us." I remember once when

Marieke and I were trying to decide whether or not to go out for a movie, and I raised the concern that we hadn't finished washing the dishes. "The dishes will always be with us," she said. And so it was for Mary. There would be plenty of opportunity for concern for the poor. But Jesus would not always be here to be celebrated. His arrest and execution were imminent, and he and Judas both knew this.

Judas is alive and well today in the economist's model of human behavior that sees us engaging with one another to seek the best pay-offs we can get. The domination of such models on our thinking is so total that it has government surrendering unquestioningly to the power of a marketplace that has, at least since Thatcher, driven poor folk into deeper poverty and has on average tripled the wealth of rich folk. No one, so the theory goes, cares about others. So the only way to get people to do things is by offering them incentives. Hence hospital management is privatized, primary care is being penetrated by corporate interests, community health services – community nurses, therapists and others working outside of hospitals – are being put out for tender, healthcare commissioning is being handled by private management consultancies, and policy-making itself is becoming privatized. According to Bob Hudson, a professor in the School of Applied Social Sciences at Durham University, writing in the *Guardian*:

> The proposed relaxation of traditional GP practice boundaries will further attract corporate giants such as supermarkets. Their tactic will be to employ salaried doctors to cater for generally healthy mobile young patients, whilst traditional practices are left to cope with the burgeoning elderly population with long-term conditions.

We're not just speaking of incentives like bloated bankers' bonuses. Millions upon millions were lost throwing incentives to

God knows who in Iraq. The money just disappeared, or wound up where we have long expected it to, in the pockets of big corporations for whom the whole incentive for making war had been to grab Iraqi oil reserves. This is just the way it is and always will be, says the wisdom of the world, and you can't do anything about it. It killed Jesus. And it continues to kill those who speak up against this blind philosophy.

In the Gospel of John, it is the raising of Lazarus that gets Jesus into trouble with the authorities and leads to his arrest. Notice that the story of the anointing of Jesus here in John is framed by the story of Lazarus, in whose home John has the anointing take place. The heady smell of the extraordinarily expensive ointment is therefore implicitly contrasted with the stench (John 11:39) of the dead Lazarus when Jesus calls him out from his tomb. This is a smell our sanitized lives usually only confront when we find a dead animal on the roadside, or when we sign on for an internship on some remote Alaskan island.

What kind of love is it that brings us into the intimacy of such smells, in caring for the elderly, for instance? When I begin to fail and reach the vulnerability of great age, what kind of love will help me eat, bathe, dress, go to the toilet? What love draws us to the intimate task of changing a baby's nappy? With what intimacy shall we honor the vulnerable, and celebrate the miracle of our shared humanity? Such extravagant love brings people like Lazarus to life, gives them the dignity of their humanity. "Lazarus, come out!" the Lord calls. The stuff of our humanity will no longer cower behind closed doors, no matter how nervous this makes the guardians of propriety.

Palm Sunday C: "The stones shout aloud"

Luke 19:28–40

The Pharisees object to the loud noise the disciples are making as Jesus rides a colt into Jerusalem. Jesus says the very stones would shout aloud if these disciples were kept quiet. What kind of stones shout? I immediately think of the current craze for hydraulic fracking of the rock beneath us to release shale gas and coal bed methane. Think of the groaning sound fracking produces when the rock is made to release the gas. Fracking also produces seepage of toxic chemicals and methane into local water tables, poisoning drinking water for humans and animals and contaminating agricultural land, which is why it is so controversial. The stones shout aloud. Do we listen? Councilors in the Vale of Glamorgan unanimously rejected an application by Bridgend-based Coastal Oil and Gas Ltd to test drill for shale gas in our area. But now the Welsh government is holding a public enquiry that might override the Vale's opposition, and Welsh Water has announced it will not participate in the enquiry, leaving the Vale of Glamorgan council without the technical support it needed to support its opposition. So it goes. The stones cry out. Who listens?

Jesus rides the colt down the Mount of Olives and across the Kidron Valley into Jerusalem. The route traces the ancient ritual journey described by Zechariah – the king's victory procession into the Holy City. What Zechariah described was once an annual event, with roots in Babylonian New Year rites. But in Zechariah's hands the ritual is no longer the old solar myth of eternal return. It is a vision of the final victory of righteousness on the Day of the Lord. And this is precisely what Jesus is picking up on in this raucous bit of street theatre. This is revelation. This is good news that is really new. The day is finally dawning. In Isaiah's words, "Our God reigns!" How will the authorities react to all this orchestrated provocation? Will they listen? Or will they silence these voices?

Paul said the creation itself longs for liberation on the Day of the Lord, stones and all. This is a powerful vision. What is being celebrated here is a victory for all things – a creation-centered or eco-centered vision of God's righteousness. Psalm 19 says the stars shout aloud, and their voice goes out through all the world. This is the song of Torah, the structure and order of creation itself, and the way we are to live. Do we listen?

Marieke and I were walking along the Cardiff Bay Barrage one sunny Sunday afternoon when it struck me what an amazing feat of engineering its construction had been. To one side of us were the mud flats of low tide. To the other the freshwater lake the barrage had created to front the vibrant life of Cardiff Bay, with its opera and art galleries and restaurants and government buildings – all this regenerating the largely disused, derelict docklands left behind by the days of coal. In the 1990s the barrage was the biggest engineering project in Europe. It struck me that engineers needed to know how physical things worked together – no cheating. It's like listening to the voices of the stones – and steel and concrete and water and the rhythm of the tides. I recalled working for the Indiana State Highway Authority one summer, standing on a soon-to-be completed stretch of the new interstate highway system that was being built across my home country at the time. The vast emptiness and the beautiful sweeping curves of the as-yet untraveled road surface again took my breath away as I imagined the complexity and precision of the engineering. You get the same almost mystical experience looking up from downtown Chicago streets at the skyscrapers, and you know why in the chapel at the Illinois Institute of Technology the communion rail is made of stainless steel. Engineers know something about Torah, the fundamental structure and meaning of things. Or should.

The Palm Sunday vision cannot be separated from a vision in

which all things are neighbors, in which we live no longer for ourselves but for others, and indeed not just for 'others' but for all things. In Habakkuk, "The very stones will cry out from the wall, and the plaster will respond from the woodwork. 'Alas for you who build a town by bloodshed, and found a city on iniquity!'" Do we listen?

Consider how many challenges to our survival as a species have to do with our denial of an essential companionship with 'all things' – poetically speaking, with the stones. We call ourselves privileged sons of Abraham. But John the Baptist said God is able to raise up sons of Abraham from the stones, yielding the kind of fellowship we need to face the massive challenge before us. Can we find the roots of our being in such company? The stones Jesus speaks of here as he enters Jerusalem are not shouting in lament, as in Habakkuk, but in celebration. They celebrate a new fellowship that encompasses the entire created order.

Maundy Thursday C: "How beautiful upon the mountains"

John 13:1–17, 31b–35

There is a painting of the Last Supper by Stanley Spencer hanging in Cookham Church, Berkshire. Jesus and his disciples are tightly seated around a table in a spare, brick-walled space that looks like the church's second-floor storage room. Their gangly legs stretch out beneath the table, their bare feet exposed below their long, white robes. I have always assumed the feet are stretched out like this to dry, Jesus just having washed them with bowl and towel.

By the time the Gospel of John was written the feast of the Lord's Supper had probably already lost its sense of hospitality and become a stiff ritual presided over by priests. I can imagine they probably even used those little individual glass cups we nonconformists insist on even when they are the kiss of death to any sense of unified fellowship. So the Gospel of John ditches the whole business of breaking bread and brings in foot washing to re-establish the kind of welcoming fellowship that Jesus had been trying to teach.

I served a church once that always celebrated Maundy Thursday ecumenically with the neighboring Anglican church. As one would expect, whatever sense of hospitality there had been in the original foot washing was lost when we turned it into high ritual. Sometimes it almost seems as if ritual was invented to put warmth and intimacy at a safe distance.

The vicar and I, dressed in white albs and stoles, washed the feet of a small group of pre-selected parishioners. They came forward to sit in a row of chairs in the chancel. I had never realized before how short and broad British feet were, compared to my own long narrow feet, inherited from my Swiss Mennonite ancestors. Needless to say, everyone had already washed their feet before the service. There was no condescension to the real world. The faith of the Church has always done it this way, dignifying what once was rough and honest with fine linen, silk, brocade, exquisite music, silver chalices, gold candlesticks and clean feet.

Unlike Peter, caught unprepared at the Last Supper by this unexpected ritual of foot washing, our church members that Maundy Thursday came with respectably washed, tidy feet. Something human gets lost in the language of liturgical formality. But it's not just the liturgy. There is something cultural going on here, too. Stephen Kern, in *Anatomy and Destiny*, writes about the nineteenth century public health movement, and how by mid-century Europeans began to become more sensitive to body odor and dirt. This change was still going on in my lifetime. The daily showering that was becoming customary in the late sixties and the overabundance of new toiletry products meant we were much less tolerant of smelly feet than we had been back in the 50s. Nietzsche, in *Beyond Good and Evil*, once said that differences in the sense and degree of cleanliness were what separated people most profoundly. They can't stand each other's smell.

So church members today are much less likely to show up smelling of mortality than they were in the day of Jesus. I remember an elder communicating a sense of shock that a member receiving communion had dirt underneath his fingernails. There was no suggestion of excommunication. But the elders decided we would not longer use a common loaf. The Church does not easily serve the unwashed.

How do we recover the raw humanity that is so often missing from church life? How do we make the Maundy Thursday experience real? Rowena Francis, writing in *Reform* magazine, reminds us of a traditional blessing: "May you always be covered with dust from the Master's feet." The dust, of course, is acquired by those who follow in the Master's steps. Back then, a sandal-wearing Jesus and his sandal-wearing disciples could not easily keep their feet clean if they were on the road practicing discipleship. We make Maundy Thursday real when we take the journey of discipleship.

At the end of the story given for Maundy Thursday, Jesus says he is giving a new commandment, that we are to love one another. Just as he has loved us, we also should love one another. The journey of discipleship is a journey of love. And washing the feet of those who have taken this journey is an act of love, and not just love, but reverence for those who have taken the journey and become covered in the dust of their mortality.

Good Friday C: "Behold the man"

John 18:1–19:42

Over the course of the long Easter weekend Jesus would be hauled before the silk robes of his day to stand trial. Think of him standing there, so silent, so powerless, dwarfed against the magnificence of the marble columns.

I always imagine him like Kurt Vonnegut's Billy Pilgrim in *Slaughterhouse-Five*. As a prisoner of war, Billy survived the firebombing of Dresden sheltered in an underground slaughter-house, and later made his way through the rubble with no boots, dressed like a joke in a too-small, crimson silk-lined, fur-collared overcoat. Its sleeves had been ripped off. Meant to flare at the waist, it was too small so it flared from the armpits. He stands silent in the smoking devastation of a strategically useless slaughter that killed twice as many as died in Hiroshima.

Pilate gestures to Jesus before the crowd and says, "*Ecce homo*." Behold, the man. Here is representative man. Billy Pilgrim. Jesus. I think of Lear out on the heath that stormy night in Act 3:

> Thou art the thing itself:
> unaccommodated man is no more but such a poor bare, forked animal as thou art.

Throughout the centuries the only way we have found to deal with such an image of representative man is to banish it from consciousness. No wonder so few show up for Good Friday services.

Here in the Gospel of John, 'the man', the one who stands in judgment before Pilate, is 'the Son of Man', the one who will be lifted up in crucifixion: "When you have lifted up the Son of Man, then you will realize that I am he," Jesus says, John 8:28.

The unaccommodated man condemned by the world's pomp is condemned precisely because of his unflinching solidarity with the will of God. "I do nothing on my own," Jesus says, "but I speak these things as the Father instructed me. And the one who sent me is with me" (John 28–29). As "the Son of Man", he embodies humanity's archetypal relationship to God.

On Good Friday the chancel may be stripped of flowers and altar cloths. But on Easter Sunday the splendor of celebration returns with a vengeance. We're onto a winner, and there is no holding back. Our worship space is perfumed with flowers. The silver has been given an extra polish. But perhaps we should ask one another what the women were asked when they came to the tomb that morning: "Why seek the living among the dead?" Why do we celebrate the resurrection with the majestic trappings of Pilate's court?

In the presence of the trial and execution of Jesus, Christianity needs to ask if evidence for the resurrection is really to be discovered among the silk and the gold brocade. Will the living Christ be found in the fragrant blossoms of the vernal equinox? Or will the living Christ be found in a society created by those who themselves have been lifted up – the condemned, the unaccommodated – who know what radical love requires?

Expressing the excruciating ambiguity between the idea of being lifted up as crucified or glorified, Jesus says, John 12:32, "And I, when I am lifted up from the earth, will draw all people unto me." The trajectory of his life is the trajectory of the life of every faithful disciple who learns to love as he has loved. The Good Friday story is our story. Elisabeth Schüssler Fiorenza reminds us that any wishing to enter into Christian community is called to relinquish all forms of privilege, whether religious, social, cultural, national or gender-based. When we are able to empty ourselves so, with Christ, then Easter happens in the life of the faithful community. If it doesn't, then as Marx once said it becomes nothing but its chocolate-coated opiate. The Church needs to learn that Easter is about what happened on Good Friday, where our new life in Christ is revealed in uncompromising clarity.

Easter C: "Why seek the living among the dead?"

Luke 24:1–12

The women come to the tomb of Jesus in the early morning. They meet these two men, who say to them, "Why do you seek the living among the dead?"

Where must we go, if we are to find the living Christ?

I will never forget when my mother first came to visit us in Wales. She arrived in the middle of April, and the first thing we did even before she had a chance to settle was to take her on a drive through the Vale of Glamorgan, where the lush green hedges and pastures speckled with primrose and skipping lambs under the bright white clouds marching across the blue sky provided the perfect picture of resurrection.

The in-flight entertainment aboard an international British Airways flight in those days always began with a seemingly innocuous little piece of propaganda for the Welsh Development Agency showing happy American and Japanese businessmen in just such a breathtakingly beautiful landscape saying how wonderful it was to build factories here in Wales. An inveterate Calvinist cynicism tempts me to suspect that any foreign manufacturers who were willing to grab the incentives offered to relocate here would just as readily abandon Wales to relocate in places like Malaysia where people are still willing to work for a pat on the back. These adverts were not appealing to loyalty. But of course I do need to join in a more affirmative support of the Welsh Development Agenda, sorely needed and a genuine social vocation for Christians who know how to do it. Wales needs jobs.

But I worry about a church that allows the marketplace to have the final word, and therefore to say that the way of the cross is doomed to futility. We live in that old chaos of the sun in which the balance sheet is the only arbiter of what is to be done:

The tomb in Palestine
Is not the porch of spirits lingering.
It is the grave of Jesus, where he lay.
– Wallace Stevens, *Sunday Morning*

So it is not just the word of science ruling out the possibility of resuscitated corpses that denies resurrection. It is also the word of the Church that allows the state to preach a marketplace that equates salvation with self-interest, enlightened or unenlightened. This is a way of understanding the world that is rooted in despair, despair that a world turned in upon itself will not and cannot change. And so we come to the tomb where they have buried Jesus, and the men we meet there say, "Why do you seek the living among the dead?"

The Church does no better than the world. If the world buries Jesus in the marketplace, the Church buries Jesus in heaven, sufficiently distant that Jesus never gets involved in criticizing the way the world works. The Church therefore paralyses itself. Its heaven disengages from any concern for the reversal of things, for justice or reconciliation or compassion for the destitute. The Church becomes an otherworldly cemetery of frustrated hopes. Why do we seek the living among the dead? Scripture asks.

Karl Marx, in *Critique of Hegel's Philosophy of Right*, criticized religion as the opiate of the people, a narcotic that enables the soul to lose itself in visions of springtime Vale of Glamorgan landscapes while the rich continue to devour the poor with impunity. And, sadly, Marx was largely correct.

But resurrection is not some comforting fiction. It is a sign that things can be different. Resurrection is about change. In Acts, for instance, Paul testifies to Agrippa that Jesus is "the first to rise from the dead" (Acts 26:23), meaning that the resurrection of Jesus was considered to be an anticipation of fulfilled hopes, a preview of coming attractions, a 'teaser' for the general resurrection to come. One might think, Paul Ricoeur says, that the resurrection itself had exhausted prophetic promise by fulfilling it. But the Church in its Easter bonnets that shouts "He is risen indeed!" needs to remember that this is not an acclamation of what is, of the current state of affairs, but an assertion of what shall be. Insofar as it is the sign that something is about to happen, the resurrection is not a closure, but an assurance in the present of a continuing hope that things can be different.

Thus the resurrection releases the creative imagination from the tyranny of the present historical moment to anticipate new possibilities: good news for the poor, release for the captives, a new way of seeing things. Resurrection, in the face of Good Friday, says it ain't finished yet.

Good Friday stands for the kind of totalization of power and perspective in communities that find it difficult to think outside the box of authorities like the sacred Hebrew texts or the imperial law of the Romans. These are communities that find it necessary to generate propaganda to maintain their hold on our lives. In the hands of those who paid good money for a position in the Temple hierarchy or in the hands of a despot like Pilate, they squash alternatives to what is. True evil, says Paul Ricoeur, is not the violation of an interdict, the subversion of the law, disobedience, but a demand for totalization that corrupts moral reasoning in an atmosphere of fear and malice.

Paradoxically, there is actually nowhere closer to the heart of Christian preaching than on Good Friday. On Good Friday, our experience of death can be like our experience of conversion, as described by William Stringfellow in *Instead of Death*:

> Conversion is the event during which a person finds himself radically and absolutely helpless. In becoming a Christian, a person sees that he is naked, exposed, and transparent in every respect – he is completely vulnerable. Conversion means the overpowering reality of one's own death, a death

> which one cannot resist in any fashion whatsoever. Conversion is so closely related to the presence and reality of death in the world and in one's own life in the world that on the day of the undertaker – when the body is carted away, submitted to the earth, and (with any sort of luck) honored by an obituary – on that day the one who is converted will know nothing, will suffer nothing which one has not already known and suffered in conversion, in one's death in Christ.

Conversion recognizes truth that is stronger than death. For Paul, at our conversion we have died and been reborn with Christ (Romans 6:3–4). Hope springs free from what the world considers the closure of possibility to proclaim new possibility. This kind of hope, which is always hope for resurrection from the dead, is what the journey of Christian discipleship through the experience of conversion is all about. We assert the deeper truth of resurrection against the false claims of those forces that attempt to control us and entrap us.

There is something about the nature of assertion in the face of contrary facts that enables us to live bravely. I remember a demonstration in a city center square in Chicago against American involvement in El Salvador's Civil War. In 1980, the Salvadoran army and security forces killed 11,895 civilians. In 1981 government forces killed over 16,000 unarmed civilians, and its military death squads would wipe out entire villages suspected of sympathizing with guerrilla efforts. Archbishop Oscar Romero was assassinated in March 1980. The right-wing oppression (today's events in Syria pale in comparison) was largely a result of US policy beginning in the 1960s, in the wake of the Cuban Revolution, to support Latin American internal security. America's silent partner role in the El Salvador Civil War became unmasked after the National Guard raped and murdered four American women in December, 1980: two Maryknoll Sisters, an Ursuline Sister and a laywoman.

Those of us who gathered in that city center square stood as witnesses to these events and to the truth of victory over death. Each of us had a small cross with the name of a known Salvadoran martyr written on it. When that name was read out, you took your cross and placed it with the others in the middle of the gathering, and everyone would shout: "VIVA!" That seems to be something like what the assertion of resurrection is all about. I find it difficult to communicate what a deep sense of solidarity I felt with these martyrs at the time of our gathering, and how our gathering was, almost literally, their continuing living presence. In the same way, I think, Christ is proclaimed to be present in the Church as the living body of Christ.

Why seek the living among the dead? The risen Christ is to be found wherever disciples hunger for a better world. Marx may have said religion is the opiate of the people, but in the same place he also says religion is "the heart of a heartless world." Christ is to be found wherever disciples refuse to take the ways of a heartless world for a final answer. We who have died and been raised again with Christ, in whom Christ lives, are called to be the midwives of new possibilities the world of buying and selling cannot imagine. We proclaim an Easter world, a world transformed by such Christ-like qualities as joy and mercy and affirmation and freedom and mutuality, despite all that threatens to entomb it. If we try to live the Christian life without these qualities, if we are timid, accommodating, afraid to criticize the world as it is, it is hard to imagine what good news we have to proclaim, and hard to imagine why the world should listen to us. We either come alive as the living body of Christ, or we close the pharmacy.

Easter 2 C: "So I send you"

John 20:19–31

The second Sunday of Easter sees the Gospel of John's version of the Pentecost story. The crucified one appears to disciples gathered behind locked doors, blesses them with peace, breathes the Holy Spirit into them and sends them out of their huddled isolation into the world.

When we hear the risen Jesus greet his disciples with the words, "Peace be with you," it is useful to recall the underlying sense of the Greek word for peace, *eirēnē*, as harmony, concord, a joined-up relationship, the tranquility of solidarity overcoming division. One 'makes' peace, through reconciliation. And of course the relationship the Gospel of John has in mind is primarily a relationship with God.

We might think of such peace in terms of that great Easter hymn, "The strife is o'er, the battle done." But peace as our relationship with God is neither the tranquility of the grave nor a cud-chewing, green-pastured bovine contentment. Peace as relationship with God is at the same time an unsettledness with those mundane, available but transitory goods in which we normally find our security. No American should feel comfortable upon learning that, in a year, the average citizen of the US consumes 50 times what the average citizen of Bangladesh consumes. In relationship to the world, what Jesus blesses his disciple with is a stressful peace. This blessing does not send us away from the world but into the world, to change it. "As the Father has sent me, so I send you."

Hence the wounds. Peace with God leads inevitably to woundedness. These things are written, John says, to teach us that the life of the one who was crucified is what life with God is all about. Those who believe this have life, not life as the world knows it, but genuine life, life abundantly (John 10:10), like the seed that dies and bears much fruit (12:24). Genuine life dies to self-interest. It is organized around the capacity to love, whatever the cost. And this happens in the flesh. Our flesh.

The vivid corporeal realism of the story of Thomas touching the wounds tempts us to imagine that the promise of 'resurrection' is about the continuation of our mortal temporality beyond death. I think, to the contrary, that the corporeal realism in the story relates to the call for the risen Jesus to be literally embodied in the flesh of disciples as the living body of Christ. This is what we mean in the Creed when we say we believe in the *carnis resurrectionem*, the resurrection of the body. This is a truth only accessible through poetry.

In John's resurrection stories, the very discontinuity of the ultra-realism against ordinary experience encourages us to read them poetically in order to discover a meaning that makes sense. They work like the kind of extended metaphor poets call a 'conceit'. A metaphor like T. S. Eliot's line in *Prifrock*, ""The yellow fog that rubs its back upon the window panes"," reveals a comparison that is and is not appropriate, but makes the kind of sense that cannot be expressed by ordinary language. By pushing a metaphor toward a realism that intensifies the tension between the 'is' and the 'is not', a conceit invites the reader into a more intense experience of the comparison. Here, for instance, in a poem by Sir Philip Sidney in the late sixteenth century, the seemingly bland metaphor of lovers sharing their hearts, "My true love hath my heart, and I have his," is made captivatingly vivid by its surprising literalization as the poem develops. Its central metaphor becomes all the more intense by pretending not to be a metaphor at all:

My true-love hath my heart, and I have his,
By just exchange one for the other given:
I hold his dear, and mine he cannot miss;
There never was a bargain better driven.

His heart in me keeps me and him in one,
My heart in him his thoughts and senses guides;
He loves my heart for once it was his own;
I cherish his because in me it bides.
His heart his wound receivèd from my sight;
My heart was wounded with his wounded heart;
For as from me on him his hurt did light,
So still methought in me his hurt did smart:
Both equal hurt, in this change sought our bliss,
My true love hath my heart and I have his.

John Updike uses the convention of a metaphorical conceit in his poem "Seven Stanzas at Easter" to make the point that the flesh of the risen Christ is, literally, the flesh of the faithful disciple. "If the cells' dissolution did not reverse," he says,

… the molecules
reknit, the amino acids rekindle,
the Church will fall.

In the next stanza, he says, "It was His flesh, ours." He makes the point here that the flesh of Jesus is our flesh. The embarrassingly literal reknitting of the molecules defines how we put flesh on the presence of Jesus in palpable acts of our own discipleship. The Church will indeed fall if we fail to become the body of Christ. "Let us walk through doors" becomes a conceit for the life that will not respect barriers to faithful action, barriers that include the impoverished world of mere things stripped of creative possibility. This is the stone that the Christian life rolls back:

the vast rock of materiality that in the slow
grinding of time will eclipse for each of us
the wide light of day.

The immortality of what fades is not what our salvation is all about, as much as we who fear death might wish. A life united with God is what our salvation is all about. Eternal life is to know God and the one he has sent (John 17:3). The wounds teach us what a world without God thinks of such a union. The realization of what all this means for his own life sends Thomas to his knees. The physicality of the resurrection, in John's poetic language, I submit, is a feature of the necessary embodiment of the living Christ in living discipleship, in us. The physicality of the resurrection, in other words, is not a matter of observable fact, as if Pilate could have witnessed it, but of discipleship, of putting Christ into the context of our own historical moment – a truth that can only be described poetically.

At the end of the day this is more than a matter of literature, or of myth. It is about the necessity of palpable action in discipleship. As Updike wrote:

> Let us not mock God with metaphor,
> analogy, sidestepping, transcendence;
> making of the event a parable, a sign painted in the
> faded credulity of earlier ages:
> let us walk through the door.

It's not easy to read this story. When John has this image of a very physical, bodily risen Jesus coming through locked doors, he is announcing that we are in the territory of a symbolic discourse that stretches not only our imagination but the choices we make about how we shall live. John says the good news of life with God is a Gospel requiring believing, a believing that shapes our choices – "the one who believes in me will also do the works that I do" (14:12). If our faith requires evidence that a corpse has been resuscitated, it won't amount to very much. What Thomas wants is not something to be believed, but something to be merely beheld. What he gets in this story is something to believe in, and to live by.

Easter 3 C: "Out of control"

John 21:1–19

Peter's decision to go fishing after the crucifixion of everything he'd hoped for has always reminded me of Ernest Hemingway's story of a young man named Nick Adams. Nick, recently returned from the devastation of World War I, travels to his family's summer place in what Americans call "the north woods" – northern Michigan. He's going fishing. We get the sense that he, like Peter, is doing this because he wants to do something he knows how to do well. The storm and the brutal confusion of war need to be put in the past. The very landscape he passes through as he travels is blackened by recent brush fires, an emblem of the burnt landscape inside Nick himself.

Nick is a fly fisherman, engaged in a sport demanding consummate skill. The story tells how he needs to force himself to concentrate on every detail, as a kind of therapy, almost, to remind himself that there is something indeed in life that he is able to master, something that can be methodical, controlled, accomplished. But every small detail of the sport threatens to defeat him, his nerves are so exhausted. In the end he needs to leave a particularly dark, branch and weed entangled stretch of the river for another day.

Peter, after his whole world has collapsed into death and absurdity, seeks out something he knows he can do. Like Nick Adams, he attempts to put a frame around himself and the familiar world of fishing, turning his back on the darkness at noon. But he catches nothing. Not only has Christ died, but something in Peter has died as well.

One Maundy Thursday at City United Reformed Church, among the shared prayer concerns, was the story from one of the Terrence Higgins staff members so bleak, so hopeless. A woman who had recently been diagnosed as HIV positive has had her petition for asylum turned down. The frame of liturgy is normally there to create a small circle of order and control in a chaotic world, but this night it didn't work. The terror came into the heart of our worship.

Jesus, whose presence Peter only gradually discerns, takes over the fishing, and the story of fishing suddenly begins to look like the story of the feeding of the 5,000 or like the grain of wheat that springs up a hundredfold.

And he takes over in other ways as well. Maybe resurrection is always like this. Jesus takes over, and Peter is no longer in control. Pilate is no longer in control. The ordinary predictabilities of our lives are no longer in control. David Cameron is no longer in control. Bibi Netanyahu is no longer in control. And so on. Everything that Jesus was ever about – non-violence, hospitality for the estranged and compassion for the despised – all this takes over and all our own petty little efforts to control the world on our own terms fall apart. This is what Paul experienced on the road to Damascus, when, he says, God "made his Son appear in me" (Gal 1:16).

The disciples, like Paul, knew that what they were experiencing was "the Lord" (John 21:12). John Taylor, who wrote *The Go-Between God*, says that to say "Christ is risen" and "Christ is Lord" is to say the same thing. When Jesus takes over as the animating spirit of your life and the life of your world, when you confess that Jesus is Lord and mean it by the way you live, then Christ is alive, in you, through you, all around you.

So resurrection and the call to discipleship are the same thing. Do you love me? Jesus asks. Feed my sheep.

Easter 4 C: "How to draw cartoons"

John 10:22–30

"My sheep hear my voice," Jesus says. "I know them, and they follow me." The Jews, he says, do not. They do not belong to his flock of sheep.

I remember being told that the sign for 'Jew' among deaf people is to trace the outline of a large nose in front of your face. This is also what Europeans in general are for the Japanese: long noses. To know this is to know how cartoons work. Whatever is different from us is funny. Does anyone recall the made-up faces of *The Black and White Minstrel Show*? Features which we think are stereotypical are exaggerated and behavior is predictable and mechanical, wooden, puppet like. Steve Martin, in *The Man with Two Brains,* moved one half of his body in a stereotypical feminine fashion at the same time that he moved the other half in a stereotypically masculine fashion. Just watching him walk across the room was hilarious. Henri Bergson said this kind of mechanical, stereotypical behavior is the principle behind all comedy. It lacks what he called the *élan vital*, the self-awareness, possibility, creativity of life.

Sixty some years ago the British historian Herbert Butterfield said that the greatest menace to our civilization is the conflict between giant systems of self-righteousness – each system only too delighted to find the other wicked, its sins giving the pretext for still deeper animosity. This is Orwell's *1984* and the Cold War, but it is still with us, and it defines the barbarism of today's neighborhood relations and international politics. The helicopter gunship, the suicide belt, the bloated arsenals of nuclear weapons, all have the same roots in human consciousness as the things that make cartoons funny. We limit one another to stereotypes, caricatures.

None of us are immune. Theologian Susan Thistlethwaite has

pointed out how racism is a chronic disease and every one of us is like a recovering alcoholic who never can come completely clean. The same has to be said for gender issues, class issues and issues of sexual orientation and the heated division of Christian and Muslim.

A critical step in moving toward greater understanding and greater authenticity involves a traumatic process of un-learning what philosophers have been calling our "grand narrative" – the story of the world we tell that finds us at its center. We need to take on board the **alternative narratives** of those whose vital humanity we exclude from consciousness simply because they speak from outside our own supporting scaffolding. How can we learn to speak to and hear each other not as caricatures but in the depth of our shared humanity? Here is an issue vital to our historical moment and to our faith.

"My sheep hear my voice," Jesus says. "I know them." For me this kind of language tells us that Jesus, in whom God was present reconciling the world to himself, is that which knows us intimately in the depth of our humanity, beyond the crippling labels and mechanical stereotypes. In Isaiah, the one who is to come "shall not judge by what his eyes see, or decide by what his ears hear," by mere appearance or hearsay or stereotypes, that is, "but with righteousness" (Isaiah 11:3–4). And because we have been known so, we can hear the Lord's liberating and reconciling voice, and know others as we have been known. For me, this is a way of living that can overcome habits of laughing at or hating those who are different. This is a way of living that can overcome divisions, even the divisions here in the Gospel of John between the believer and 'the Jew' in which what is good and redemptive is so sadly buried and obscured. Habits of mind that make the other mechanical and predictable put us as well as the other among that which is dead. But the Gospel shouts a quickening "Tabitha" to us: "Stand up and live!"

Easter 5 C: "Play it again"

John 13:31–35

Jesus asks his disciples to love as he has loved. Our faith is what we do, and what we do is what Jesus did. Jesus says whoever receives our ministry receives him, and whoever receives him receives the one who sent him. Here is the essential continuity in the transmission of God's love.

The task seems overwhelming. I remember MP Diane Abbott learning to play the piano in four months in a television documentary series called *Play It Again*. Diane's task was to practice scales and technique until the awkwardness of her untrained fingers fell into place and she was able to play Chopin's *Prelude in E Minor* before a large public audience at St Martin-in-the-Fields with some semblance of the composer's intentions.

Her experience parallels much of the journey of discipleship, doesn't it? Jesus shows his disciples how to wash a guest's feet, and the resistance to what is unaccustomed comes with equal struggle. The disciplines we practice in loving as Jesus loved carve channels of peace through the rough terrain of our inexperienced hearts so that the grace of God can flow through them unimpeded. The good news can continue to be published unchanged through our own lives and by our own prayers. It can continue to be published with its original clarity even while, as in Diane Abbott's performance at St Martin-in-the-Fields, there may be the occasional minor disaster. The message gets through.

The discipleship required for such high fidelity is the bedrock of the Christian life. If we remain content to be part of an onlooking audience and never embrace the opportunity to perform our Christianity, if we hesitate to practice the disciplines of Christian living that enable Christ to come alive in us and through us, then, as Paul says, 1 Corinthians 14:14, all our preaching has been in vain and our faith has been in vain.

Christians are commissioned to be God-bearers to the world. Of course there is always the possibility of betraying our commission. The story of the betrayal is inserted here in the midst of this great affirmation of continuity. Why Judas betrayed Jesus is never made clear. All it says is that Satan entered him. Like Iago in Shakespeare's *Othello*, Judas' betrayal seems without motive.

However we interpret his motivation, we can at least say that his betrayal constitutes a failure to love as he has been loved, and a failure to embody the love of God. In Judas, the Gospel comes to a dead end. By contrast, there is a sense in which discipleship represents a kind of continuing resurrection, Christ coming alive in the world through the fidelity of discipleship.

That doesn't mean we are condemned to blind, repetitive obedience to the past. The Gospel doesn't work this way; neither does piano playing. The piano student will never amount to a hill of beans if she simply remains content to ape the skills and the techniques of her tutor with mechanical precision. To be an artist she has to make the music come alive, interpret it from the deep resources of her soul and in relation to the moment of performance, in the spirit of communicating with a particular time and place. In making the music live in this way, the pianist is not betraying what she has received, but fulfilling it. It's the same with the Gospel; it has to be good news for real people in real situations today. It needs to live, as Peter, in Acts, found his own tradition coming alive for a new day when in a vision he heard the words, "Kill and eat!"

Easter 6 C: "Raise the public average"

John 14:23–29

One of my worst habits is wishing I could be 18 again, or maybe even 10 or 11, to be able to do it all over again, but wisely and more responsibly. I would spend more time practicing my scales, be more diligent in learning languages and reading more books instead of hanging out by the soda shop's juke box trying to look cool. But my wishes have never been granted, and I remain the same person I have always been, still hanging out trying to look cool instead of practicing my scales. Our prayers are often like such wishes. We want the hard facts of life to be whisked away. For Christians who pray this way Jesus is imagined as a kind of wish-granting fairy godmother, watching over us, answering our wishes, finding us parking places in busy city centers.

Jesus knew this about us. So he said, he promised, "I am coming to you." He knew that we are creatures who wish. He knew how hard it is for us to face the pain of departure, of death. He knew our longing wish that the world might not be as it is. He knew us through and through, and in the Gospel of John's long "farewell discourse", he answers those deepest longings with comforting assurance.

Jesus takes our wishes seriously. But he also takes reality seriously.

He says, Keep my commandments. The word "keep" here means guard, watch, hold onto, cherish, protect my commandments with your life. Do this, he says, and I am with you. And God will live in you as God lives in me.

Now there is nothing all that mysterious about this. What Jesus is saying here is that OUR faithful lives, OUR daily activity will constitute the presence of Christ in our world. And this will come naturally to us. Those who love me will keep my word, he says.

So we don't have to wish for Jesus to come back into our lives. All we have to do is read this book, know what it says and take it seriously.

It sounds simple enough and practical. But to be honest many readers find the words of the Gospel of John difficult. John is not like the other Gospels. He's not so interested in action, and his Jesus is deeply reflective and a bit long-winded. Reading a lesson from John in Sunday morning worship can easily put people to sleep. His style seems ethereal, as if he had been influenced by the writings of the ever-popular Khalil Gibran, whose writing sounds like wisdom, but I can't quite figure out what he means.

Gibran, who wrote in the early twentieth century when there were plenty of momentous issues to write about and writers burned to live on the cutting edge of the historical moment, turned out sentiment clothed in an already passé late-Victorian style and the cadences of the Authorized Version. Beauty, he muses, is "eternity gazing at itself in a mirror." "What is death but to stand naked before the wind?"

John isn't like this at all, when you get down to what he is really saying. There is no foggy-brained mysticism in the Gospel of John. The presence of Christ is found where the rubber hits the road in our discipleship. John may require a bit of patience and discipline to understand, but once you get there you see he calls a spade a spade.

One time while visiting San Francisco I stayed with a friend who served on the staff at Cameron House, the Presbyterian neighborhood center in Chinatown. Downstairs they had one of those rooms where they kept the tools, the paint pots, jars of nuts and bolts, that sort of thing. And it really wasn't in any better order than my own garage back home. But they had a sign that read:

EVERYTHING IN THIS SHOP IS IN THE RIGHT ORDER. WHEN YOU FINISH WITH A TOOL, MAKE SURE YOU

> RETURN IT TO THE RIGHT SHELF. THE NATIONAL AVERAGE FOR RETENTION OF WHAT IS READ IS 17%. PLEASE DO YOUR PART TO RAISE THE NATIONAL AVERAGE.

Answering the question, "Lord, how is it that you will reveal yourself to us, and not to the world?" Jesus says, in essence, that he is present in those who keep his word. Now you can't get much more down to earth than that. It's not about wishing things could have been different. It's about discipleship. It's about doing what Jesus did, being animated by the same spirit that animated him. So let the word become flesh in you. Love it, cherish it, guard it. Jesus will come to you.

Ascension C: "Bearing witness"

Acts 1:1–11; Luke 24:44–53

In a book called *Leaving Church*, Barbara Brown Taylor tells of her first experience as a solo pastor, when she was no longer anyone else's assistant. She was now, she says, the one church members rang when they landed in Accident and Emergency, or found a loved one lying lifeless on the bathroom floor. She was also the one they rang when they were furious about the financial committee's report or the way the Sunday school teacher had spoken to a child or why the coat rack had been removed from the church entrance.

In theological college Taylor had heard about how people naturally transfer to you the feelings they have about someone who has played a significant role in their lives, but is now missing – a parent, for instance – especially when they are feeling vulnerable or emotionally at sea. Old feelings of dependency or anger erupt from somewhere in the mist of the past and become focused on the minister. Now this was happening for real. It was not just something in a textbook on pastoral care.

Taylor's central role as minister of the church made her the focus of disembodied emotions that cried out for embodiment, emotions that once belonged to another relationship – a childhood dependency, feelings of anger, frustration, and experience of abandonment. All this had little to do with her, and at that point in her ministry she was too inexperienced to know how to resist.

In the story from Acts we see the apostles staring into just such an empty space. The space that was now empty had been defined by this Jesus, who had taken the lead in healing the sick, forgiving the sinner and raising the dead. Now he was gone forever.

The apostles were in an emotionally vulnerable state. Who

would fill their emptiness? Would they fall into a crippling relationship of emotional dependency with the next two-bit would-be-savior they might meet, someone who had the complimentary emotional need to be depended on, to have a fan club, a community that would adore him, praise him, sing hymns to him? This isn't what happens in the Book of Acts. The apostles grow up. Emotionally mature, they take on the ministry of Christ, preaching, healing, forgiving sins, raising the dead. Christ came alive in them, as Christ comes alive in our ministry today.

Taylor says that for many people God is like a parent who has walked out of their lives, and they feel this absence painfully. As a minister, she unconsciously stood in for this absent God, took the blows intended for him and received much of the adoration. Filling in that space, we can feel much more powerful that we actually are. It feels good to be needed. The people's emotional needs can feed our emotional need to feel important. But this keeps the people themselves in spiritual infancy, as in the old Sunday school hymn:

> Jesus loves me, this I know
> For the Bible tells me so.
> Little ones to him belong:
> We are weak, but he is strong.

In the rest of the world, such a need to be needed passes for strong, dependable leadership. We've all heard the praise of church secretaries, treasurers and organists who have served faithfully for decade upon decade. In reality, when attention isn't given to mentoring others to take over, this pattern of leadership cripples congregations, robs them of power; it is a prime factor in the death of communities like our churches, because it never allows the people to grow up.

By contrast, a new generation of leaders is built the same way

Jesus built the leadership of the apostles, by delegating, by getting out of the way. The Gospel invitation to every Christian is thus the same as the commission given to the apostles at the Ascension: to become mature adults, to become the presence of Christ in the world. And equip a new generation of disciples to do the same.

Do you remember the movie *Black Orpheus*, a Brazilian film from 1959 retelling the Greek myth of Orpheus and Eurydice? Here in the film Orfeu, as he is called here, plays guitar (the soundtrack, by Antônio Carlos Jobim and Luiz Bonfá, contains songs that became bossa nova classics). He has told the two young boys who follow him around throughout the film, Benedito and Zeca, that his guitar playing causes the sun to rise in the morning.

At the end of the film both Eurydice and Orfeu have died. Benedito insists that Zeca pick up Orfeu's guitar and play so that the sun will continue to rise. Zeca plays, and the sun does indeed rise, as Orfeu had promised.

In much the same way, I think, the disciples of Jesus took up his guitar and, from the Ascension on, made sure the sun would continue to rise.

Easter 7 C: "Shared bread"

John 17:20–26

Jesus prays that his disciples "may all be one" (John 17:21). I think a good example of such oneness is the Catholic Worker movement. They band together around common concerns for poverty, social justice and non-violent activism.

On St. Patrick's Day 2003, two days before the invasion of Iraq, four Catholic Workers from Ithaca, New York, who came to be known as the "St. Patrick's Day Four", entered a military recruiting center to carry out an act of non-violent civil disobedience. They carefully poured their own blood around the vestibule. The four were tried in county court a year later on charges of criminal mischief. Nine of twelve jurors voted to acquit.

A year later, the US government decided to retry the four, now on charges of conspiracy. The trial was held in Binghamton, New York, in the first and only federal conspiracy trial arising out of civil resistance to the Iraq War.

Facing up to six years in prison and $250,000 in fines, they were cleared of the most serious charges, but were convicted of misdemeanor charges of damage to government property and entering a military station for an unlawful purpose. All of them have been released from prison now after serving their terms.

Their action in solidarity with the Iraqi people is what the Gospel of John means by the oneness of discipleship. As Christ is one with the Father, in solidarity of purpose, so the disciples find their unity in being one with Christ and the Father together, and are sent into the word as Jesus was, to love as he has loved, without counting the cost.

Daniel Berrigan, SJ, one of the "Catonsville Nine" tried for resistance to the draft during the Vietnam War, has talked about his own non-violent witness as a witness to the resurrection and as the Word made flesh. These have been important themes in my own thinking throughout my own ministry. Whether we are talking about standing up for the discarded and forgotten in political engagement and protest or sitting down at the bedside of the dying, accompanying them in silence, allowing the Word to become flesh in our own lives creates new forms of community and a new humanity. The trial of the St. Patrick's Day Four reminds us that sometimes such faith-in-action can get us into trouble. But this is the kind of unity we are called to live out. Liturgically, this is still the Easter season, and this is an Easter unity.

In one of his books Berrigan writes that his study of the biblical book of Job taught him a few important things: a summons to live humanly in a bad time; a faith that verges on despair, that looks that dark eminence in the face and is not turned to stone; a faith that survives a battering of accusations and insults; a faith that would not be put to silence. This is the kind of faith that thrilled me in my younger years. Now, all I hear at church conferences is talk about how to save the old institution from terminal collapse. My bones get rigid just thinking about it.

Well, some church get-togethers don't do this to me. City Church once hosted a delegation of clergy from Syria. We spent the afternoon listening to the stories of Catholic and Orthodox and Congregationalist Christian communities working together with Muslim neighbors to respond to the overwhelming needs of refugees who have flooding into Syria fleeing conflict in Lebanon and war in Iraq. This, too, was a unity born of the unity we have with Christ. I often wonder where these church communities are standing in the horrific stories of violence emerging from their country today.

At another conference I heard of a church with a special ministry to isolated people like ex-offenders who often live alone and with few social skills. They were invited to meals in the church hall where church members sat among them, interacting with them, and they were invited to members' homes. Gradually, these people came out of their isolation, learning to take on responsible, interactive roles. A new Christian community emerged from the simple symbolic action of table fellowship.

When I speak of the Word taking on flesh I am not just speaking about political activism, but also the simple acts whereby the inner spirit of what we do as a church becomes real in our ordinary lives. That's all. It's the invitation to become real we hear from the Gospels every time we open them to be read in our midst. Life together – it's the reality of what it means to be human.

Pentecost C: "Ardor or order?"

Acts 2:1–20; John 14:8–12

Before I was interviewed for the church in Birmingham where I served for nine years, I was asked to meet the elders and be interviewed at another church. They were a charming lot. Their morning service was traditional, staid Presbyterian, but their evening service was charismatic, spontaneous, wild and spirit-filled. The interview did not go well. They asked me things like whether I believed Muslims go to heaven. I was more concerned about how I could manage the extraordinary diversity of this community.

When I got back to Cardiff I asked John Humphreys, then our synod moderator, why they had asked me to interview at this church. Surely they had known that the church was charismatic.

Yes, we knew that, John said. But you were the only one we knew who moved your body when you sang hymns. We thought you might fit in.

It is important to remember that the Pentecost story in Acts is about a Jewish festival that celebrated the time Moses received the gift of the law on Mount Sinai, a gift that the people celebrated with joy and overflowing emotion, much as Pentecostals do on Pentecost.

Luke says the apostles gathered there in Jerusalem for the festival were overtaken with the whoosh of this enthusiasm and began speaking in tongues, a mode of worship that was already known in the pagan Gentile community, and would increasingly become a feature of the Jesus movement as it spread through the Gentile world. Actually, this aspect of Luke's Pentecost story is probably a reading back into this early story of something that actually only began to be experienced when the Jesus movement began to move out into that Gentile territory. This didn't bother those who were there in Jerusalem for the festival that day. They were overcome by the Spirit anyway.

Some thought they were drunk, but Peter explains their enthusiasm not just as common religious mania or the God-frenzy Plato spoke about, but as recapturing a prophetic dream for a new world, an end-times story. He explains it in terms of the death and re-birth of Jesus, and in terms of the death and re-birth of the believers in baptism, a people re-born, their lives filled with the living presence of God as promised on the Day of the Lord. As Paul would say, now is the time of salvation.

That is what we see here, Peter says. Not drunkenness, but the hoped-for living presence of God. It is not self-indulgence, certainly not drunkenness, but an enthusiasm for a new way of life, like the enthusiasm proper to this festival, the enthusiasm for the way of life given to God's people in the Torah.

The passion and liveliness of Pentecost has immense appeal. Abraham Lincoln once said he liked to see a spirit-filled preacher preach like he was fighting bees. But the point of this story from the Book of Acts ultimately has less to do with the big whoosh of spiritual ecstasy than it does with the way this whoosh unfolds in building up a community.

We hear how these Galilean followers of Jesus begin to communicate with Parthians, Medes, Elamites, Libyans and Mesopotamians and so on by speaking in their own languages. The Parthians, Medes, Elamites, Libyans and Mesopotamians and so on were amazed. This has never happened before. It was as if a bunch of American or British tourists had suddenly taken the trouble to learn to speak the languages of the countries they were visiting, rather than expecting everyone else to speak English. So a new fellowship is created, one that has honored the outsider and affirmed the stranger. By the end of the chapter we hear that this polyglot group of people is meeting regularly together and sharing their possessions with all according to need.

Thus the order and structure of this early church community

was something that emerged naturally from the Pentecost enthusiasm, and indeed from its Jewish roots.

The point we need to take away from this story is that the Church needs to keep the enthusiasm and the structure together. Too often they get polarized. But here we see an enthusiasm that is an enthusiasm for others and an emerging structure that is a people-centered and a person-affirming structure of life together. Sometimes the Church in its passion for passion forgets that there are important things like concern for social justice or religious literacy or the kind of good church order that prevents a community from falling prey to the emotional manipulation of rabble-rousers or the imbalanced power of a bully pulpit.

Sometimes, on the other hand, the Church in its passion for order loses its warm spontaneity and becomes stiff and cold. It is no longer fed by the spirit but finds the spirit a threat, and blocks it, like a blockage in the arteries.

The necessary union of ardor and order has not been well managed in our tradition. I remember when I was an undergraduate bringing home a stack of old 78 rpm records I'd found in a second-hand shop. I played a dance number called *The Black Bottom* and my parents, the staid Presbyterian minister and his wife, got up to perform a dance that required them to turn around at one point and bump their bottoms together. The next record I played was *Silver Threads Among the Gold*, which brought tears to my father's eyes. He made me turn it off.

Neither the joy of the dance nor the deep sorrow for loss seemed to be part of the black-wool cerebral dignity of our public religious life. Paul's admonition that everything be done decently and in order had a stranglehold on passion. The fact that my body moved while singing hymns probably owed more to the influence of Elvis Presley than it did to Scottish Presbyterianism. We mocked people who spoke of their conversions, so I didn't experience anything like conversion myself until I had been in ministry for maybe fifteen years, and I only let down my guard enough to pray from the heart when evangelicals came to join the churches I served, and their passion for God's compassion struck something in me that had been missing.

Before that, my prayers were either glib poetic reveries or starchy High Geneva affairs modeled on seventeenth century prayer books. I discovered one can only really pray when God's concerns start burning in your heart, and then a living formal structure erupts naturally from some place within you. I think this is a process similar to what we see in the emerging Christian community in the second chapter of Acts. God's passion for the needs of neighbors burned in their hearts, and the early Christian community was the natural result, a living prayer.

To be filled with the spirit of Pentecost is to be overwhelmed by the presence of God, so that what God does, we will do. It defines how we act. Isn't that what Jesus means, when he says, in John 14, that we who believe in him will do what he does, and do even greater things than he has done? Jesus, here, says those who have seen him have seen the Father. The Father is in him, and he is in the Father. And we, who have opened our lives to God's Holy Spirit, find that the Father is in us as well, and we are in the Father. It shows in what we do.

Opening ourselves to the Father's presence in our lives has profound implications for the life of the Church. It means church structures will be spirit-filled – well managed and well-equipped for the work of ministry in such ways that maximize participation, give voice to the voiceless among us, break down patriarchal power structures and make the institution a community permeable to the gifts of the world around it.

In a church that seeks communion with the God of the cross through communion with those whose lives are torn apart and robbed of spirit, we need to provide experiences of jubilation that are alternatives to a heartless marketplace world. That means more festivity and lucidity in our liturgies, less by-the-book formality. We need to bring song and celebration and aestheticality to our gatherings as alternatives to the world of materialism, consumption and exploitation. The Pentecost Spirit can also give increased profundity to our Good Friday solemnity. The task is to live richly.

Harvey Cox, in *Fire from Heaven*, says, "In some respects, especially in their emphasis on the need for personal experience of God, [Pentecostals] were closer to the Protestant liberals of the day than they were to the fundamentalists. The difference was that while the liberals like to talk about the importance of religious experience, the Pentecostals seemed to generate it." And yet we must guard against thinking that experience of God is only found in our worship style, a mistake often made. The experience of God must be found in the total shape of the Christian life.

Living as those filled with the presence of God implies living with a profound and lively enthusiasm for God's agenda. This means an enthusiasm for ethical living, enthusiasm for justice, enough oomph to challenge the power and affluence of a society that disregards the marginalized. Pentecost is far more than being able to move with the music. It's moving with the music of God's coming kingdom.

Trinity C: "Dancing with Wolves"

John 16:12–15

Ten women every day are coming forward to Cardiff police to admit they are victims of domestic violence, and given the reluctance of most to open up this can of worms, this number is probably only the tip of an iceberg.

This nasty social reality reminds me of the conversation I once had with a friend visiting from Canada about a sermon he'd once preached on spouse abuse.

Domestic violence was rife in the isolated rural plains communities of Western Canada where Murray was serving as a minister. German and Ukrainian farmers had settled here, where they experienced a double isolation, not only from their extended families back home but from one another on the vast emptiness of the plains.

Women tied to ultra-traditional domestic roles on remote farms often lacked the driving skills that would get them out of a bad situation and the small farm towns where everybody knew everybody hardly offered shelter to escape to. The women were trapped.

The Church was the only institution offering anything resembling social services, but it was the Church, with its steady diet of sermons on wifely obedience and the biblical principle of male supremacy, that left battered and abused women trapped not only in a bad marriage but also in a sacred universe of meaning that in fact formed an important element of the trap itself. It was a trap that couldn't be questioned. Wives, submit to your husbands.

So when Murray dared to speak up, he was speaking up not only against domestic violence but against the religious beliefs of his community. It was religion speaking out against religion, belief challenging belief.

What he had to do was to reach back into Scripture to recover that original core of loving kindness that needs to inform the interdependence of human relationships and build up a compassionate community that could be called the body of Christ. In order for his church community to become a safe place for an otherwise invisible company of battered women, Murray first had to change the way his people read the Bible, change what they understood about the nature of God, and change how they interpreted their own discipleship. This was a tall order.

All religions have a tendency to become sacred clothing for whatever domination system is going at the time, because the religion we practice is always pretty much a product of our own hands, and therefore idolatrous by definition.

Paradoxically, Christianity has a tendency to succeed best, says Philip Jenkins, "when it takes very seriously the profound pessimism about the secular world that characterized the New Testament." The Gospel of John, much loved by a more conservative corner of the Church for its born-again language, is nevertheless scandalously clear about the embeddedness of the sacred in what it means to be truly human. You know the Spirit, Jesus encourages his disciples, "because the Spirit abides with you and will be in you." "The world," Jesus says, "neither sees nor knows the Spirit."

This tension between the world and the human being embodying the presence of God is what Murray had to get across. "My thoughts are not your thoughts," says the Lord in Isaiah 55, "nor are your ways my ways." The faithful disciple has to stand apart from the world in order to discover the depth of what it means to be human, to be created in the image and likeness of God. Though we are sent into the world (John 17:18), we are not of the world. Marieke and I used to remind each other of this when we lived in a posh, leafy middle-class suburb in Birmingham.

The vision of God's presence in Jesus that is also present in us is what the Church eventually came to mean by the Trinity, a doctrine proclaiming the presence of God not only remote and beyond us, but also present in the human life of Jesus of Nazareth and by the Holy Spirit present in us, binding together the Christian community.

Of course the Trinity is not always understood in this way. Too often the Trinity has been used as a central feature of that dysfunctional authoritarianism so problematic in Murray's community, as a cudgel to mark who is in and who is out, who is orthodox and who is not.

John Calvin, for instance, had the physician Michael Servetus burned at the stake for refusing to believe in the rather wooden and mechanical understanding of the Trinity that prevailed at that time. During his trial Calvin called him a "villainous cur" and when he was burnt at the stake they used slow burning green wood so that it took him a good three hours to die. This was our spiritual ancestor John Calvin who did this. To be fair, Calvin only wanted him beheaded. It was the Geneva Consistory that wanted the slow death.

Religion needs to speak up against religion because, simply put, religion kills people. Writing from prison shortly before his execution, Dietrich Bonhoeffer observed that faith has always had a tendency to become arid, rigid and tribal, a means of making our basest prejudice, privilege and power into sacred duties.

What we need is something like a religionless religion.

In the future, Bonhoeffer says, people would be called to speak the word of God in new ways, ways that will change and renew our understanding. The new language we will use to describe what it means to be Christian will shock people, but it will also overcome them by its new vitality.

It is a tall order to change the way we read the Bible, change what we understood of the nature of God, and change how we practice our own discipleship. This is a tall order indeed. What language can we borrow, as the hymn says, to make sense of God today? Jesus invites us to be sons and daughters of God alongside him. Does that sound scandalous? It's biblical (John 14:12). We will do what he has done, and even greater things, as new occasions teach new duties.

Many who have jettisoned the old language as unworkable, unjust, perhaps even destructive, have found themselves cut adrift in a sea of vague liberalism, or even secretly and sometimes with immense guilt have found themselves identifying with atheists, unaware that those who first followed the irreverent, liberating words of Jesus were themselves vilified as atheists.

In the name of their faith, these early 'atheists' refused to accept the prevailing faith of their day. Sometimes it feels like you have murdered your parents to take this step, it can be so traumatic. But at the end of the day it enables you to live richly and authentically together in hope as God's people. It has always been the prophet's role to point out the failings of the orthodoxy of the day, and point toward an unexpected future.

Proper 4 C: "No empty world"

Luke 7:1–10

I'm told that my grandfather's cousin, Arthur Hays, who taught Church History at McCormick Theological Seminary from 1909 through 1945, drilled generations of students in Williston Walker's maxim that "Christianity entered no empty world." Christianity is inextricably embedded in culture, emerges from particular historical contexts and in transmission is received in the terms another cultural context is able to understand.

My grandfather himself was a creature of the culture that was fading in the post-war years of my coming-of-age. While we were listening to Jerry Lee Lewis playing *Whole Lotta Shakin' Goin' On*, he would be listening to the polkas and waltzes they played on *The Lawrence Welk Show*. I never saw him not wearing a tie, unless he was in his night shirt. He had little tolerance for children. I remember having to be sent upstairs on Wednesday evenings when the Bortzes came over to play bridge with my grandparents. I watched, silently, through the rails of the banister, a world in which I was unwelcome. I hate the game of bridge to this day. He was, as my mother described him, a "Goldwater Democrat", a dyed-in-the-wool member of the Democrat party, an inescapable family heritage, who nevertheless seemed more comfortable with the values of the ultra-conservative Senator Barry Goldwater. He used to joke, when anyone dared to ask him to do anything, which was rare, that he was a man accustomed to authority. "When I say to one, 'Go'," he'd say, "he goes; and when I say, 'Come', he comes" (Luke 7:8). And then he would go do whatever was needed to be done. His black wool Western Pennsylvania Presbyterianism was not without a rare note of humor.

The story of the centurion who sends for Jesus to heal his slave is a story of faith that stretches across two cultures. It won't do to explain away the discomfort we feel with the centurion's slave being described as precious in the sense of being valuable (*entimos*). Nor do we feel easy that the centurion's perception of the power of healing is expressed in terms of military authority. We remain conscious that this is a land and a people under military occupation.

The centurion, who loved the Jewish people, lived beyond his own culture, but at the same time remained tied to that culture. I recall the words of Johnny Shawnessy in Ross Lockridge Jr.'s novel, *Raintree County*. He was, he said, "a notch or two above the other hicks, but a hick nevertheless." We remain inescapably who we are. Here in Wales, I will always be an American, and in some ways only really discovered what it meant to be American once I had lived here in Britain for a few years. My friend and seminary classmate, Randy Campbell, spent his internship year in the rusted-out steel-mill town of Gary, Indiana, which by then had become a devastated community of unemployed African Americans. The primary learning he took away from that year, he said, was that he learned what it meant to be White.

The literary context of our story is the Sermon on the Plain in the previous chapter, which has loving one's enemies as a central focus. What links our story with that story is the concern Jesus had there for the disciples doing as they were told. "Why do you call me 'Lord, Lord', and do not do what I tell you?" (Luke 6:46). Here in the centurion Jesus finally finds someone who knows what it means to listen. "Not even in Israel have I found such faith, " Jesus says.

What follows our story is the story of raising the widow of Nain's son from death, which Luke's readers would have recognized as an Elijah story and therefore, I think, an end-times story, a story about that time when the dead rise to life. This is reinforced by the next episode in Luke, when John's disciples come to ask Jesus if he is "the one who is to come," and Jesus tells them to simply tell John what they have seen, the standard end-times experiences of the blind who receive their sight, the lame who walk, the lepers who are cleansed, the deaf who hear, the dead who are raised to life, the poor who have good news brought to them (Luke 7:22). The literary context of our story seems to imply that the story of the centurion evokes the last-days' motif of the gathering in of the Gentiles, which starts in earnest in the Book of Acts.

But any standard commentary on Luke is going to tell us this kind of stuff. What I find interesting is this movement between one culture and another that Luke is playing with here, adding details highlighting such an interest that do not appear in Matthew – the whole business of the centurion's relationship to the Jewish community, for instance. Underlying Luke's ongoing concern for the way the story moves from Galilee to Jerusalem to Antioch to Rome is a story of cultural transition that is also an end-times story and a story of death and resurrection.

Mircea Eliade, in *From Primitives to Zen: A Thematic Sourcebook of the History of Religions*, says, "One of the outstanding characteristics of traditional societies is the opposition that they assume between their inhabited territory and the unknown and indeterminate space that surrounds it." Home is the world, the cosmos. What is not home is not cosmos, space inhabited by ghosts, demons, "foreigners" and the dead. Eliade quotes from the Ngaju Dayak of southern Borneo a vision of what it means to die:

> And I have myself become like a cast-off stone, never to return.
> I am like a clod of earth thrown away, never again to come home.

This is not an expression of despair, Eliade says, but simply a farewell to the world of home, the ordered cosmos, spoken from the world of death and meaninglessness.

The journey outside one's cultural bearings, I suggest, not just for Eliade's traditional peoples but also for those of high Roman culture, can be like the experience of dying. It can become like a descent into meaninglessness, anomie, total disorientation. This is also the common experience of conversion – a profound experience of disorientation followed by a gradual reconfiguration of one's world. This is the kind of experience Paul refers to when he says he has been "crucified with Christ" (Galatians 2:19). It is an experience of death and it is also an experience of resurrection. It is no longer Paul who lives, but Christ who lives in him (Galatians 2:20). No one goes through conversion without the experience of being thrown away like a clod of earth, never again to come home. Even though, inescapably, we carry ourselves with us. On a personal level, this is what the end-times story looks like in Luke. In the whole sweep of the Luke-Acts narrative, it becomes the experience of an entire people.

But certain people always get left behind. I recall the servile mentality of so many of the local people in the town where I attended university. When someone asked them something they didn't quite hear, they didn't say, "Pardon?" Stuck in a traditional authority structure, they automatically assumed they were being asked to do something, and habitually said, "Do what?" The authority of the Christian chain of communication is not an authority that requires servility, or an unquestioning response to an order from above, but a new kind of authority that requires the close listening (the original meaning of 'obedience') that is important in mutuality, forbearance and solidarity, the kind of listening that enables us to love our enemies.

Certainly, it has been the experience of my generation, or a significant company of my generation, to move into a new kind of Christianity that would be unrecognizable to my grandfather, faithful elder of the Church though he was. Yet even while I continue to fight to defend the vision of Christianity that so many of my generation, up against the powers and principalities of this world, have defended with their lives, I see this Christianity of ours evolving still. I fail to comprehend the heavy shepherding that so often passes for Christian leadership today. I actually find it distressing.

Proper 5 C (Corpus Christi): "This is my body"

Mark 14:12–16, 22–26

When we were in Ely, Cardiff, Marieke and I took in three children from the local children's home, siblings, aged 11, 10 and 5 at the time. I was serving three churches in the Ely Pastorate, and they wanted to go with me everywhere, to every pastorate event and service. James, the middle one, loved to hand out the hymn books.

In Wales the United Reformed Church, mostly former Congregationalist churches, practices open communion. Children are welcome to participate fully. When I was growing up we couldn't participate in the Lord's Supper until we had been confirmed. We had to understand what was going on, to discern the body of Christ, as Paul said. Apparently after having been grilled in the Geneva Catechism and formally received into the Church at the age of eleven, we knew what we were doing. Later in the States there had been a massive campaign across the Presbyterian Church advocating the presence of *baptized* children at communion (the idea of the covenant community gathered at table was still important). But in Wales, well, it was all family. For me, this relaxed attitude toward rules and structures was a breath of fresh air.

Only two or three weeks after we took in the kids, the Pastorate was to celebrate communion at an evening service. The two eldest piled in the car to accompany me (Rachel was being told a story and being readied for bed). They hadn't been baptized, and although the eldest, Tina, had been attending our Sunday school for about a year, they had almost no previous experience of church. So I was furiously explaining to them the meaning of the Lord's Supper, the story behind it, the sharing of the bread and the cup that creates community, the coming together as if we were the 'members' of the body of Christ. They kept saying, impatiently, "Yes, we know. We understand. Don't worry." Ha!

When we arrived at the church the vestibule was crowded with people who wanted to check notes with me about this and that, share urgent pastoral concerns, and so on. Among them was Bill, one of the regulars from the Ely Residential Hospital for people with learning difficulties. He, along with the others, was trying to tell me something, but with his somewhat garbled speech and my bum hearing, I couldn't make it out. Tina said Bill was telling me it was his birthday. So I greeted him warmly with "Happy birthday, Bill!" A moment or two later he was trying to get my attention again. Tina explained that he wanted me to look at his new shoes – they were splendid, white, unscuffed. A birthday present.

The elders commandeered me and sequestered me in the vestry to cut a few last minute deals and have vestry prayers before the start of the service. There was not a whole lot of time to think or prepare myself for conducting worship. When the time finally came in the service for the communion and the breaking of bread, I discovered the bread Bronwyn had baked was tough and crusty. I tore it apart as best as I could, but it stayed in fairly large chunks on the serving plates. The congregation would have to manage as best as they could.

Bill was sitting in his usual seat on the front row. When the plate came his way, his eyes lit up and he grinned widely. He must have imagined that this was another birthday present. He took one of the larger pieces, maybe four or five inches in diameter, and passed the plate on.

Had Bill "discerned the body of Christ"? Probably not. But the rest of that evening's congregation had. They knew that all had been welcomed, all the family had been joyfully included in this feast. Everyone was smiling. Bill's participation had made it a very special moment for them. There was no brokenness remaining in our community that evening. Why had I been so worried about the kids?

The feast of Corpus Christi is designed to bring greater visibility and broader participation in what our Catholic brothers and sisters call the "Eucharist", the feast of thanksgiving for the life the Lord has given us. The feast of Corpus Christi has its origins in a thirteenth century Augustinian Sister named Juliana of Liège, who petitioned the hierarchy to give a higher public profile to the consecrated bread, the 'body of Christ'. Her efforts came at a time when few lay people ever received the communion elements, and the service itself was shrouded in high altar mystery and secluded in clericalism.

As a matter of fact, the term 'hocus pocus' dates from this time, as a play on the Latin words for 'this is my body' in the communion service, 'hoc est corpus meum'. It wasn't just that 'hoc est corpus' *sounded* like 'hocus pocus'. In the lay imagination what happened up there on the altar in changing ordinary bread into the body of Christ seemed as fanciful as the magician's tricks performed at the annual county agricultural fair.

The feast of Corpus Christi went a long way toward changing all that. At the feast of Corpus Christi the consecrated wafer of bread called 'the host' would be put on display and adoration of the host would join the disciplines of popular piety. The host would be carried in celebratory processions through the streets. In England, on the feast of Corpus Christi, the procession came to include plays performed on wagons by members of local craft guilds, plays depicting the drama of faith from Adam to Doomsday, centering on the life of Christ, plays that brought the inherent drama of the body of Christ into the life of the people – all the struggles, the conflicts, the victories and the joys of the story of God's grace.

The emphasis struggled to remain on the host itself, the consecrated wafer of bread at the heart of the communion service. But the unavoidable significance of this bread as the embeddedness of Christ in the life of the people continued to bloom. The parades, the celebrations, the community theatre, all this highlighted something that gathered the people and transformed them into a people of faith, and still does. At the same time that Corpus Christi celebrated the consecrated host as the body of Christ, it elevated the way that broken bread brought together the whole people of God. How ordinary bread became the living body of Christ was no longer the mystery it had once been.

For Paul, the body of Christ was first and foremost the people who broke bread together, gathered as Christ's risen, living body. The whole project of building a compassionate community worthy of the name of Christ re-emerged from the heart of the symbolic nature of the host so publicly embraced and fêted on Corpus Christi. So it was no great step to make when John Calvin, the granddaddy of our Reformed churches in the sixteenth century, spoke of how in the sharing of this bread we cleave together in Christ. The bread forms a people, and in the faithfulness of the people we find the real presence of the body of Christ.

The bread shared binds us together as Christ's new body. Shared bread creates the Christian fellowship that gives itself to the world just as Christ has given himself to us. We, this fellowship, become the living body of Christ for today. So the body of Christ is of course more than bread alone. In a sense the body of Christ is what the bread *does*. When we hear the words of Jesus in the communion service saying "*this* is my body," perhaps we ought to think of the word "this" as referring more to the gesture of sharing the bread than to the bread itself. The body of Christ is constituted in acts of giving and sharing. This is what the festival of Corpus Christi needs to parade through the streets today.

We are the body of Christ not just in the breaking of bread, not just when we gather for the Lord's Supper. When we sit down to share the Lord's Supper, *and* when we gather to share our concerns in prayer, when we share our food in a potluck supper, share our wealth at the offertory, when in our meetings we share in decision-making, and perhaps most importantly when we reach out beyond the church to share our life with a world in need, in all this we are coming together as the body of Christ, living not for ourselves or to push our own agenda but living for one another and for the world, as Christ's living body today. This is exciting stuff that looks forward to what the world can be, and the church that hasn't discovered the outpouring of new celebrative music for the Lord's Supper, particularly that flooding in from an international community of Christians, and joyful, new, ecumenical liturgies has been missing out, and, in Paul's words, failing to discern the magnitude and wonderfulness of the body of Christ today.

We are the body of Christ in what we *do*, and do together. The body of Christ is a living body, not static like a club with dues and membership rosters, but a process of being Christ together for the world.

And there is more depth to this mystery yet. It is not just something that *we* do together that constitutes the body of Christ. It is not something we do but something that Christ continues to do in us and through us, for we who have been crucified with Christ have also been raised with Christ, and it is no longer we who live, but Christ who lives and acts in us.

When I was young my father, a Presbyterian minister, told me the story of Graham Greene's novel, *The Power and the Glory*. A priest is on the run as the only priest left in a country that has outlawed religion. He is an alcoholic and an adulterer. But that didn't take away from the validity of the sacrament he was called upon to celebrate for those who still believed and were in need, my dad said. Because the bread and the wine were the gifts of God for the people of God. The clergy were only God's plumbing. The transforming power of this feast is not diminished by the broken and compromised lives that celebrate it. It belongs to the people. All the people. The breaking of bread continues to be Christ's gift to us, something that Christ continues to do through us and through these ordinary elements of table fellowship in bread and wine.

Proper 6 C: "A time to break down, and a time to build up"

Luke 7:36–8:3

Robert Frost has a poem called "Mending Wall":

> Something there is that doesn't love a wall,
> That sends the frozen-ground-swell under it,
> And spills the upper boulders in the sun,
> And makes gaps even two can pass abreast...
> ... at spring mending-time we find them there.
> I let my neighbor know beyond the hill;
> And on a day we meet to walk the line
> And set the wall between us once again...
> ... He will not go behind his father's saying,
> And he likes having thought of it so well.
> He says again, "Good fences make good neighbors."

In Luke Jesus take the side of that "something" that doesn't love a wall.

It is at the cross, in Luke, that Jesus says, "Father, forgive them, for they do not know what they are doing" (Luke 23:34), overcoming the kind of conflictual ideological certainty we find both in Roman authority and Jewish apocalyptic with a neighboring reconciliation. In Ephesians 2:14 the crucified Jesus is "our peace." He has "broken down the dividing wall" of the hostility that divides us, so that we are "no longer strangers" (Ephesians 2:19). How does the Church, today, break down the dividing walls that prevent us from being neighbors – the walls of class, creed, race, gender and gender orientation, wealth and so on?

There is a certain hunger of the heart in this Gospel that creates neighbors in a world of estrangement. The women who follow Jesus have been "cured of evil spirits" (Luke 8:2). Other stories of neighbor-making are events of healing, exorcism, reconciliation, forgiveness overcoming social distance. The story of the 'woman in the city', for instance, the woman of unsavory reputation who bathes the feet of Jesus with tears and costly ointment (Luke 7:36–50), is a story of the hungry heart overcoming estrangement. The estrangement is overcome as Jesus receives her hospitality, just as in the sending of the 70 the missionary task is to receive the hospitality of those they encounter. Jesus says to his host, Simon the Pharisee:

> Do you see this woman? I entered your house; you gave me no water for my feet, but she has bathed my feet with her tears and dried them with her hair. You gave me no kiss, but from the time I came in she has not stopped kissing my feet. You did not anoint my head with oil, but she has anointed my feet with ointment.
> – Luke 7:44–46

Elisabeth Schüssler Fiorenza, in *Jesus and the Politics of Interpretation*, speaks of those who hold positions of power – slave owners, husbands, the elite, freeborn educated and propertied males, etc. – as engaging in a logic of "othering" understanding others as "not" (e.g., not white, not male, not civilized, etc.). The classic instance is Luke's story of the Pharisee and the tax collector, where the Pharisee prays, "God, I thank you that I am not like other people: thieves, rogues, adulterers, or even like this tax collector" (Luke 18:11). And, of course, there is Simon the Pharisee's remark about "what kind of woman this is" (Luke 7:39).

Replacing the model of the 'other' with the model of the 'neighbor' recognizes the validity of another person's culture and basic humanity and transforms the life of the perceiver. Again, to be a neighbor is not a matter of geographical or social proximity, but of an openness to others that transcends the ego's need to dominate and enables us to receive and return the gift of hospitality. A logic of 'neighboring' overcomes a logic of 'othering'.

Schüssler Fiorenza suggests we ask what our own social location – our own group identity – has to do with our relationships to others. Where are we on the pyramid of domination? What is our socio-political, religious, cultural, economic location, and how does it relate to our social group's ability to be a neighbor to others? How does it compare with that of those who pick our tea leaves in Sri Lanka, mine our diamonds in Sierra Leone or, in Kenya, package up fresh vegetables for overnight delivery to our local Waitrose? How do we 'neighbor' the world's diverse population?

Neighboring is a form of hospitality. It is a common experience to show up at a sparsely attended church meeting and ask, "Where is everybody?" Letty Russell, in *Just Hospitality: God's Welcome in a World of Difference,* reminds us that this is the kind of question that is proper at *any* of our meetings. We need to ask who is missing, in the sense of asking who are those whose voices are not being heard. Who are those either inside or outside the institution who remain outsiders? Our unity can be an easy unity, when it excludes women, for instance, or turns a deaf ear to minority ethnics. The kind of unity that welcomes all persons and seeks unity through hospitality is hard work. A just hospitality "is an expression of unity without uniformity. Through hospitality community is built out of difference, not sameness; there is no 'either/or', 'right/wrong', 'win/lose'."

Deborah Beth Creamer, in *Disability and Christian Theology: Embodied Limits and Constructive Possibilities,* challenges the kind of 'either/or' thinking that divides the disabled from the non-disabled. Her "limits" model is an alternative to the standard medical and minority models for understanding disability:

> The limits model differs... in that it does not attempt to divide participants into one of two categories (either disabled or non-

> disabled) but instead offers a new way to think about what disability is... Where the medical model begins with an evaluation or assessment of limitations, the limit model begins with the notion of limit as a common, indeed quite unsurprising aspect of being human. Unlike the minority model, the limits model avoids categorization and instead encourages us to acknowledge a web of related experiences, suggesting, for example, that a legally blind person may in some ways be more similar to a person who wears glasses than to a person who uses a wheelchair... Key to the limits model is the recognition that 'disability' is actually more normal than any other state of embodiedness.

The woman in the city's hungry heart opens up new, neighboring communities that disclose a deeper truth, the kind of truth addressed, for instance, in Stephen Levine's work, *Who Dies? An Investigation of Conscious Living and Conscious Dying*. We must not be estranged from what it means to be human. Death, too, is a neighbor.

Proper 7 C: "The sound of silence"

1 Kings 19:1–4, 8–15a; Luke 8:26–39

Mount Sinai is the place where Moses, and Elijah after him, met God. The closest I ever got to Mount Sinai was on a visit to a Bedouin friend in Israel who teaches at Ben-Gurion University in Be'er Sheva. Along with his extended family, Ismail lives in the Bedouin village of Lakiya, some miles outside Be'er Sheva. Speaking to him some weeks before I arrived, I told him I really wanted to see Mount Sinai. He said I obviously had to learn a thing or two about the local geography. Though Be'er Sheva is known as "the gateway to the Negev desert," he said; we were nowhere near Sinai.

A friend of mine, Ivor Rees, has been to Sinai. He says the 3:00 a.m. climb up 1200 ancient steps nearly killed him, but his was the first group to arrive that day. He'd been looking forward to the mountaintop stillness of the sunrise, but that was not to be. As he and his companions waited for the dawn, they were joined by a couple dozen charismatic pastors from Korea whose Hallelujahs and loud, cacophonous praying allowed no space for quiet meditation. And it got worse. The intensity of their worship was taken up by an equally enthusiastic group of Muslims from Port Said.

Elijah, on the run from Jezebel, finds his way to Be'er Sheva and from there makes it to Sinai, where he finds God in the silence rather than in the big wind or the earthquake or the fire.

I didn't have to find Sinai to experience what Elijah did. The boisterous wind, earthquake and fire were only too present. My friend Ismail had bought a video player which he couldn't get to work, so several times over the fortnight I stayed with him we had to return to the electronic gadgets shop where they kept trying to fix it. The shop was in a large shopping center on the outskirts of Be'er Sheva called, simply, "BIG". Its name shouted from a huge rotating sign mounted on a tower soaring above the cluster of megastores. It was, as one might have imagined, decorated in red, white and blue and (white, five pointed) stars, to remind us of the bigness of all things American. The shops were almost all American chain stores, including a massive McDonald's, a visual reminder of the huge amounts of cash the USA pours in to shore up this country. Is the voice of God to be heard here, in the bigness?

And of course all this contrasted sharply with the poverty of the Bedouin communities. Israeli authorities won't allow a post office in Lakiya, so you have to walk or catch a lift all the way into Be'er Sheva to get your pension check. The Lakiya shops, run from the front rooms of residents' homes, are basically illegal – violating Israeli-imposed zoning restrictions. Lakiya, a village of 8,000, is one of the resettlement communities populated by Bedouin who had been removed from their traditional lands in the years following 1948. It got water and electricity only a few years ago. Most Bedouin villages, illegal in the eyes of the Israelis and under constant threat of Israeli bulldozers, lack such provisions. Israel had nationalized all land in 1948, even though the Bedouin community's ancestors had lived in the Negev for countless generations. Meanwhile the same Israeli muscle is felt across other Palestinian communities. Israeli settlements, illegal under international law, continue to be built on traditionally Palestinian land, with government subsidy, and impoverished Gaza is forbidden building supplies and even such daily necessities as toilet paper. Is the voice of God to be heard here, in big Israeli muscle?

What is big and powerful has always had a certain attraction. Like the booming club music young people like to play full blast from their car speakers, it has a power to distract us from ordinary life. But in the end, there is something insidious here in the attraction of bigness that ultimately destroys us. In the time of Jesus it was the Roman occupation that made all the big noises. It can literally pull us apart (that's what 'distraction' means), as it did the young man of Gerasa, possessed by a demon named "Legion". Political and economic occupation can get inside us like this, as possession in need of exorcism.

In contrast to what is big and noisy, like Caesar's boisterous trumpets or British soldiers with assault rifles trooping the color to raucous military band music, the voice of God is heard in the silence. The voice of God speaks in the silence of the cross ("Why have you forsaken me?") and in the voicelessness of the broken spirit, in those who mourn, those who hunger for righteousness, those who make peace. Perhaps these, like Moses, Elijah and Jesus himself, will always be on the run or on the cross. They have not been distracted from where they need to be.

Proper 8 C: "Pilgrim through this barren land"

Luke 9:51–62

Once while driving back home along a twisting, narrow road from a retreat center in North Wales, I was listening to Handel's Messiah, to the tenor air: "Ev'ry valley shall be exalted, and ev'ry mountain and hill made low." Looking at the breathtaking beauty of the landscape through which I was driving, I thought, is this really what my soul desires?

I remember driving down from Chicago to the small town in Indiana where I had grown up, to be with my father when he was taken into hospital, critically ill. It's a straight shot for four hours through a flat landscape, corn fields on either side stretching unbroken to the horizon. When I finally got there, and met my mother at my father's bedside in the hospital, we could see that he was OK as long as the hills and valleys of his heartbeat were marching along across the screen of the monitor. When they flattened out, we knew we had lost him.

Rough landscapes can be appealing. I had been serving as a Presbyterian minister in Chicago when I received a phone call from John Morgans, then moderator of the National Synod of Wales, asking if I would be interested in serving with the United Reformed Church here. I knew nothing about Wales at the time, but John was very convincing. The call was to serve three struggling churches on a sprawling council estate on the west side of Cardiff, one of which needed to be rebuilt after arson burnt down its hall. It grabbed my imagination. I said "Yes." It was just three weeks after my father's death that we made the move.

The advice Jesus gives to his would-be followers sounds brutal and harsh. "Follow me," Jesus says. And one, who has just promised to follow him wherever he may go, asks if he might first go back to bury his father. "Let the dead bury the dead,"

Jesus says. "No one who puts a hand to the plow and looks back is fit for the kingdom of God."

Following Jesus can be like the journeys the Desert Fathers took, spiritual seekers who walked away from a settled urban life in the Nile Valley into wilderness. Leaving the compromising security of home, they chose to live unencumbered. They put themselves on trial, struggling against loyalties that held them back from living as Christ, choosing to live more ethically, honestly, and compassionately.

I worked on the staff of McCormick Theological Seminary for three years following graduation, before I was ordained to the ministry in 1981. Every morning as I walked up the stairs to my office I passed a stained glass window made by Jesse Halsey, who had taught at McCormick a generation earlier. The window depicted Bunyan's Pilgrim, from *Pilgrim's Progress*. Seeing the window every morning as I mounted the staircase became a fleeting act of prayer focused on vocation, a pilgrimage I was conscious of delaying. The isolation of the academic community was becoming increasingly uncomfortable for me. I think there is something in the human spirit that seeks to be put on trial, to be tested, to break away into the insecurity of the unfamiliar.

The song, *Guide Me, O Thou Great Jehovah*, popularly known as *Bread of Heaven* here in Wales, is a Welsh favorite. They even sing it at rugby matches. Everyone knows it, loves it and can sing it by heart, Christian or not. Guide me, a pilgrim through this barren land, it sings. The hymn speaks of life as a pilgrimage, being carried safe to Canaan's side, singing songs of praise against the ever-present reality of death. Singing it brings me back to those early morning glances at Halsey's stained glass window, and what that window came to mean for me.

The journey of Christian discipleship is just as much at odds with the jumble of public life today as was the intensity of desert emptiness at odds with the green, vibrant culture of the cities of the Nile in the days of the Desert Fathers. Why would any sane person in this day and age come to church? Crossing the threshold to enter a church is a deliberate, emotional act, a pilgrimage, a seeking after something different. Sometimes those of us who grew up in the Church tend to forget this. We have domesticated the Church. It has become a comfortable, chatty sort of place. We need to remember that the Church cannot afford to be just another location for predictability and settledness, cakes and tea. A living church demands a certain instability, an adventuresome exploration of new perspectives, a sense of serious pilgrimage.

If the Church is a company of those who have left home, it is also a company of those who, paradoxically, have left church. Our only purpose for gathering is to be scattered. Once the Church becomes an end in itself, domesticated, seeking its self-preservation and stability, it starts to fester. The job of the Church is to live out the life of Christ, the life for others.

Church can become too much like home. So leaving church, like leaving home, is what the Church is all about. The whole point of our gathering Sunday by Sunday is to give us the courage to scatter. At its very heart, Christianity has to be a journey toward life lived together with neighbors in need and destitute strangers and with enemies. That means Christianity needs to be a journey away from those loyalties that tempt us to betray people, a journey away from things like family loyalties and family values, a journey away from racial and national loyalties and loyalties to denomination and creed and church buildings and favorite hymns. Christians who respond to the call of Jesus to leave church need to be able to question such loyalties, to grasp the freedom to explore and grow.

The high point of our communion liturgy, after all, is an act of breaking bread that enables stranger to come together with stranger, forming a new family and a new table fellowship that did not exist before. The whole point of sharing in this broken loaf and this poured out wine is to follow the trajectory of God's love into the godforsaken, hungry world to which Jesus himself came, to be broken and poured out. This is the central paradox of Christianity. Only in such brokenness do we find ourselves safe on Canaan's side.

Proper 9 C: "Be the change you seek"

Luke 10:1–11, 16–20

I was walking down Queen Street in Cardiff one day when I spotted a van with a sign saying "FREE ICE CREAM". I couldn't believe it. I had to stop, but when I asked the young man if his sign really meant what it said, he explained that you had to buy something from The Top Shop first. If you brought your receipt from The Top Shop, you could get a free ice cream.

The gimmick reminded me of the suburban Chicago church whose large fleet of coaches prowled the streets of the Chicago metropolitan area offering free ice cream to any kid who would attend their Sunday school.

Jesus sends out his disciples to teach and heal. But I don't think he is interested in marketing strategies to promote a brand-name Christianity. Many churches today are borrowing business models, using marketing techniques to bring in more customers. We need to remember that we as a people are not sent into the world to corner a market but, as these disciples were, simply to receive the hospitality of those we meet, and so affirm them, and in such affirmation liberate them from all the forces that are at work to manipulate them and entrap them.

That's why we are sent out unencumbered by anything but the image of a cross on which a young man from Nazareth was once executed. We are not sent out as well-equipped marketing agents to rope people in or to get them to buy our product, but to be vulnerable to them, to allow their needs to guide us and their hospitality to welcome us. Jacques Ellul, in a chilling book called *Propaganda*, says it is impossible to adapt the predatory strategies of the marketplace without becoming like that predatory marketplace ourselves. We think we can, but we can't. Jesus says he sends us out among wolves, but he doesn't expect us to become wolves ourselves.

I and a colleague once visited one of our churches in the South Wales valleys. We spent our time listening to their history, their experience and their dreams, and sharing with them what we had heard them say about possibilities for discovering a renewed vitality. At the end of the day their only question remained the one they started with: "How do we get more people to come to our services?" Sadly but understandably, this is where most of our small, struggling churches will start, and end. Do we simply give up on them for their lack of imagination? Do we resign ourselves to the terminal decline of an institution that, let's confess it, has had its day? We can always come in loaded with slickly designed programs for building up the congregation. Or we can come as Jesus would send us, unencumbered, vulnerable among the vulnerable, simply seeking hospitality, seeking what is Christ-like among them and helping them see that and name that.

Our denominations ask us on a regular basis and in an interminable offering of new campaigns to take up the work of evangelism. Will we sign on to the latest ideas for church revival, advertising campaigns, learn to put on non-threatening smiles and open our arms, adopt programs that look suspiciously like an offer of free ice cream, with the hidden agenda of simply getting more people attending our services? Is our evangelical agenda a membership drive? Won't the public see through this? A young divorcee once told me how difficult it was to meet men. "They take one look at me," she said, "and they know right away that I am desperate." So it goes with the Church's publicity campaigns.

Jesus sends the seventy as laborers for the harvest and as sheep among wolves. Their vocation takes the form of what we can call "mission in reverse" – simply seeking the hospitality and table fellowship offered by the people they meet, allowing themselves to be guests. This prepares the way for Jesus in Matthew's sense that whenever we welcome the stranger, we welcome him (Matthew 25:34–36).

I get the term "mission in reverse" from Claude Marie Barbour, who teaches at the Catholic Theological Union in Chicago and with whom my wife worked in inner city ministries in Gary, Indiana, and in Chicago's Kenwood-Oakland and Uptown neighborhoods. The key idea of mission in reverse is the willingness of those of us who go in mission to become listeners and learners when we are tempted to be proclaimers. The agenda is pure Gospel, the correction of power imbalance, as in Paul's teaching, "He became poor, so that by his poverty you might become rich" (2 Corinthians 8:9). So mission in reverse becomes particularly critical with poor and marginalized people, or when we enter into a culture that is not our own and, similarly, need to learn to listen. By listening to and learning from others, by affirming them, genuine, uncluttered relationships can be established and the dignity of the other is enhanced.

Ministry is often understood in terms of what the minister can do for people, how the minister, as an expert, can shape the community. I came up against such an understanding in an interview as a candidate for a pastoral studies lectureship with the theological faculty at the University of Aberystwyth once. After sharing with them what the various communities I had served had accomplished, they wanted to hear what I myself had accomplished, and they would not accept the role of enabling through listening and learning as a proper answer. The common model of leadership here was once explained to me by one of my elders. It's your job to tell us what to do, he said. And it's our job to tell you we're not going to do it.

By contrast, there can be a dialogical model of ministry that aims to do things with people, to enable them to discover in themselves what they can do for themselves, all in a relationship in which they find themselves affirmed. This is the kind of healing and liberating ministry Jesus sent the seventy to practice, and it worked. As the seventy return from their mission, Jesus tells them he saw: "Satan fall from heaven like a flash of lightning" (Luke 10:18). Mission in reverse allows the other to be the leader of the relationship. A new, genuine community takes over the usual institutional hierarchies when mutuality happens, when the minister can be ministered to, for instance – a mutuality that simply cannot happen before mission in reverse has taken place.

Juan Luis Segundo, in *Faith Conversations with Contemporary Theologians,* reminds us that evangelism must not be confused with wanting Christianity, or the Church, to be accepted. The authentic message of evangelism is liberation in specific historical situations – where there is hunger, discrimination, even real slavery – rather than in some merely abstract sense.

The opposite of Segundo's "authentic message of evangelism" is found in the aphorism from Latin antiquity, *homo homini lupus* (humans are like wolves to each other), popularized in modern European thought by Thomas Hobbes and built on by Freud in his 1929 *Civilization and its Discontents.* Will this become the Church's motto, too? Rather than adopting the predatory behavior that defines the economic practices our secular world lives by so unquestioningly, we are called to go into this world as lambs. As Gandhi said, we are to be ourselves the change we want to see in the world. Any evangelical enterprise worthy of the name Christian will leave its self-interest behind, and seek to build up the Church by building up others.

Proper 10 C: "This is your life"

Luke 10:25–37

Life is made up of other people. You know that old television program called *This is Your Life*? They'd put some poor soul on a couch in front of a camera and start reminiscing about life, saying, "Do you remember so-and-so," and sure enough so-and-so, who hadn't been seen for forty years, would appear from the wings and there would be hugs and tears and reminiscing. Life is made up of other people.

That's the point Jesus is trying to make in this story, the story we call "The Good Samaritan". The lawyer sums up the commandments as loving God with all you've got and loving your neighbor as yourself, and Jesus says do this, and you will live. This is what life is all about. In a very real and fundamental sense we cannot love God and not also love our neighbor, so these commandments are one and the same. Acknowledge the claim your neighbor makes on your heart. Your own life is, by definition, about other people. Life lived alone is no life at all.

To the lawyer's question, "Who is my neighbor?" Jesus tells a story that says more about how to be a neighbor than it does about who our neighbor is. Life is made up of other people. To live is to be a neighbor, Jesus says. Do what the good Samaritan has done. Do this, and you will live. This is your life.

But did you ever notice that this is not what the lawyer wanted to know? The lawyer had asked what he must do to inherit eternal life. Jesus was telling him how to live now, like the Christian Aid motto, "We believe in life before death." The lawyer wanted to know about his life after death, and how to guarantee it.

The question of how we inherit eternal life is the quintessential religious question, isn't it? And it is a question that comes out of a very privatized understanding of religion – religion as security for me. Death will not touch me. God will protect me, if I live, as the lawyer does, a clean, upright life, obeying all the rules. What rules do I have to follow, the lawyer asks, to inherit eternal life?

The priest and the Levite in the story represent the religious mandarins responsible for maintaining the strict standards by which their people keep themselves clean, untainted from the world in holy isolation. It is because they are concerned about their own eternal life that they cannot cross to the other side of the road. The laws of religious purity forbid them touching someone who might be dead.

Wouldn't it be great if we just obeyed a set of rules and nothing ever had to change? We would feel so protected and safe. The free trade that makes rich countries rich and grinds poor countries into deeper poverty would never have to change. The oil industry-driven politics of America could keep on pursuing its war on terror with impunity, grabbing control over more Middle East oil reserves, and the oil industry itself could continue to cut costs by compromising safety requirements in deep sea drilling. You could keep on beating your wife. Nothing would ever have to change. We would never have to change. There would be no falling in love, no conversion, no death. We would just sit here in our Victorian pews like pieces of non-biodegradable plastic, and never have to change. What do we have to do to make this happen? the lawyer asks.

But the rules we live by are meant to be broken by the cries of others that pierce our hearts and deepen the level at which our conscience operates. Here is the clue to an answer to the lawyer's question. The eternal life he desires is simply what the Bible says it is: life with God, which is inseparably full of other people and full of change. And more: real life is life engaged honestly with the reality of death. Unless we learn to die like the grain of wheat planted in the ground, we remain, sadly, only ourselves. But we shall be changed, Paul says, willy-nilly, in the twinkling of an eye.

Eternal life is changed life and life lived now, not a reward that comes after we die, and certainly not a reward of never-changing continuity. Those who hope only for their own self-preservation have missed the point. They have never learned to hope as Christians do, for others. Jesus invites us to forget about our ultimate destination, and think about other people.

One of the characters in Jean-Paul Sartre's play, *No Exit*, says, "Hell is other people." And for too many of us, Hell is indeed other people. We won't cross to the other side of the road because we worry about what might happen to us. But the Bible says Heaven, as a metaphor for life with God, is other people. The life we are called to is a life that crosses to the other side of the road, not concerned about what might happen to us. We are invited to think like Jesus. We are to worry not about ourselves but about what might happen to the guy in the ditch if we don't cross over. Those who seek to save their lives will lose them, the Gospel says. Those who risk them for others will find them. Eternal life is not a reward for living this way. This way of life is eternal life. This is the life we are promised. This is the way of life we are invited to start living now.

Proper 11 C: "Distraction"

Luke 10:38–42

A City United Reformed Church member told me Nora Morgans once opened a Bible study there cautioning that the book had been written by men, for men. This fact is nowhere more evident than it is in Luke's story of Mary and Martha, in which Mary is praised for sitting silently at the feet of Jesus while Martha is chided for being distracted by the kind of domestic activity traditionally the province of women.

Many women will find themselves identifying with Martha. So from the viewpoint of women's experience, the story throws up difficulties that traditional (male) readings ignore. Martha, in the story, is distracted by much servicing (the NRS and NIV translation of *diaconia* as "work" is misleading). Women traditionally find their vocation in serving, in managing the household. They do the cooking and the laundry, the shopping, the cleaning, the childcare.

The early church seems to have benefitted strongly from the leadership of women, and this seems to have much to do with women's tradition role in offering hospitality. In the early church *diaconia* referred specifically to eucharistic service in the house-church, and therefore to ecclesiastical leadership in general. As the early congregations were house-churches, and eucharistic services in these early house-churches were, literally, community feasts, one can easily imagine why women took a predominate role. Hospitality was both the medium and the message of early Christianity. As Elisabeth Schüssler Fiorenza points out in "A Feminist Critical Interpretation for Liberation: Martha and Mary" (*Religion and Intellectual Life*, 1986), such service included proclamation and other forms of apostolic leadership as well as ordinary hospitality.

Paul's letters testify to the many women who were evangelists, organizers, hosts and leaders of house-churches. Martha herself appears in this story as one of those leaders, and welcomes Jesus as an equal here, and the kind of hospitality she represents is central to Paul's understanding of the Church as the barrier-breaking body of Christ. The late Letty Russell speaks of such a gospel-oriented hospitality as going beyond a cheerful welcome, charitable benevolence or tables loaded with fried chicken and three-bean salad. In *Just Hospitality*, she uncovers an original sense of the Church's hospitality as true partnership with the "other" in a divided world. True hospitality is inseparable from doing justice.

So why is Martha's service seen as distraction? Why is Mary's listening in silence praised as the better part? Part of the answer can be found in looking at how Martha represents the place of women in today's church, which consists largely of communities of women attending to the needs of a largely male leadership.

A colleague of mine, while a student, spent a summer working in a church in Massachusetts. To meet equality laws, they appointed twelve deacons and twelve deaconesses. The deacons dealt with masculine things like finance and church policy. The deaconesses had the flowers and kitchen, etc. They met periodically as the Joint Church Council. What happened in fact was that the deaconesses met and decided what should happen, then spoke with the deacons' wives at women's meetings, and the wives talked to their husbands. The deacons then came up with brilliant ideas which they shared with the deaconesses at Joint Church Council. This is the way it goes in so many churches. Martha arranges the flowers and runs the lunch club and organizes the jumble sales and organizes the bake sales and coffee mornings and church dinners. She helps out with the pastoral visiting, cleans and presses the communion cloths and prepares the communion elements and washes up afterwards.

In the larger frame of the story Mary's silent devotion, sitting at the Lord's feet (10:39), is, for Luke, the "better part" that needs to inform what women's Christian service (*diaconia*) is all about – disempowered silent adoration. The Lord (*kyrios*) is at the center. Elisabeth Schüssler Fiorenza says Martha's service seems to come into question as distraction only in the context of what she calls Luke's *kyriarchy*, the culture of male dominance that so quickly took over the Jesus movement to give us the Church we have today, dominated by males, with hospitality no longer at the center of its theology.

Men run our churches. But paradoxically, in Wales, and no doubt other areas of what used to be Christendom, real men don't come to church. No wonder. Disempowered, domesticated women have a virtual monopoly on what it means to be Christian – and who wants to be like them? Church has largely become a women's club, a social backwater for women content to serve a male hierarchy. This is a corruption of true hospitality and a corruption of the Gospel.

Though we all value what we call good workers in our churches, here in the story the Marthas of the Church get no praise. It is the Marys who sit silently at the feet of Jesus listening passively to his teaching who are praised. Here is the seedbed of the inward-looking spirituality, the numbing of social consciousness, the greeting-card-verse theology, the emasculated sentimentality of today's church. The story is a prime example of patriarchal dehumanization, when you really think about it.

Do we ever wonder what it might have been that Jesus is teaching here, as Mary sits at his feet listening to him and Martha busies herself in the kitchen? Maybe he is telling the story of the Good Samaritan, telling Mary how the clergy can and often do lose the plot, which calls us to risk crossing to the other side of the road to offer hospitality. Maybe Jesus is telling Mary about inviting himself over for a meal at Zacchaeus' house, who responded not only with joyful hospitality but with a whole re-direction of his life. These are stories of justice as hospitality.

These are lessons the men and women in our churches today

need to learn. If we lose our focus on this kind of teaching, then all our work is in vain. The reading from Amos gives us a critique of a community that has lost the proper focus of the Church's work: Amos speaks of a people who can hardly wait for the Sabbath to be over so that they can get back to overcharging and cheating their customers.

The same principle needs to be applied to the story of Martha and Mary itself. To what extent has it lost the focus on God's central compassion for the marginalized? To what extent has the very community that needs to have such teaching at its core become an institution that obscures such teaching?

One last thing. When Martha comes to Jesus to complain about Mary, Jesus says, "Martha, Martha." One of my favorite books is *Dealing with People You Can't Stand: How to Bring Out the Best in People at Their Worst*. It suggests that when someone is being awkward, at a church meeting, for instance, repeating their name like this will calm them down. So just remember. When someone repeats you name like this, "Martha, Martha," you know you are being patronized.

Proper 12 C: "Seek and you will find"

Luke 11:1–13

I have a poster at home with a photo of someone slouched in a chair staring vacantly at nothing in particular. The caption says, "The trouble with doing nothing is that you never know when you are finished."

Luke's version of Jesus' teaching on prayer is a spur to get up off the couch and make things happen. Seek and you will find. Knock on the door. Desire something, and go for it. I have a T-shirt from an Islamic source that says, in Arabic, "Seek and you will find." There is nothing parochially Christian about this encouragement. No one, from investigative journalists to astrophysicists, is ever going to find anything unless they first get up off the couch and start looking. Seeking starts with the suspicion that the real truth is yet to emerge.

Now many people have problems with this kind of advice about prayer. The blunt fact is that you don't always get what you pray for. Probably most of the time you don't get what you pray for. Reality often reduces our human desire to smoke. Whatever this piece of scripture means, it has to accommodate this blunt fact.

The problem here is a certain model of prayer embedded in patriarchal power relationships. We are powerless children. God is the Big Daddy who satisfies our every wish. Patrick Richmond discussed in a *Reform* magazine article the cognitive science research that says such an understanding is innate in children, and not a product of religious indoctrination. Humans are naturally prone to belief in a Big Daddy God – what John Calvin called our inbuilt sense of divinity.

Richmond wants to argue that just because such models have been programmed in human brains since the Pleistocene, it doesn't make such belief untrue. But that is not the point. The problem is not so much a question of truth as it is spiritual maturity. We can get stuck in such a dependency relationship and never grow up.

A classic example of the kind of piety that believes fervently in the power of prayer to deliver the goods is found in the cargo cults of Papua New Guinea. Apparently the World War II era experience of supplies being dropped by parachute inspired and gave shape to religious communities praying for riches to come from heaven like parachuted cargo. Ask, Jesus says, and you will receive (Luke 11:9). The hopes of these people took shape in the anticipation of a new millennium of prosperity, dignity, freedom and peace. What a joke, Richard Dawkins would say.

There is another model of prayer on offer that takes seriously our standing as adults. Jesus invites us to grow up, to take our places around his table as brothers and sisters, as companions in ministry. Here, we are reminded in the first instance that prayer is communication with God, in touch with what Tillich called the ground of being, that fundamental source of life itself and the actualization of life in reconciliation, spiritual maturity and dynamic, selfless hope. To pray is to be absorbed by the desire that God be all in all. To pray is to learn to desire what God desires.

So ask. Of course we must ask, ask out of this deep relationship to what we most wonderfully and finally are. Don't just lie there like a lump waiting to be served.

To ask as Jesus invites us to ask is to throw out everything we know about prayer. Don't 'pray'. Habits of the heart are important. But if 'prayer' is a duty to be performed at certain hours in prescribed words and perfunctory rites, don't do it. Collections of canned prayers as resources for the spiritually dry – best sellers in Christian bookshops – can re-inspire, but when they become a crutch they become counterproductive.

What we need is something much more like the devotional models that emerged in the Reformation era: diary keeping, for instance, not records of appointments or what you had for breakfast but irregular, deep reflection emerging from moments of crisis and intensity like John Donne's "Batter My Heart, Three-Person'd God". It is in the heat of this forge that your very soul is being tried by the choices that are put before you to act on your deepest hopes, prayer book at hand, scriptures at hand, trusted companions at hand, but at the end of the day most terribly on your own before God, struggling with who you will be and what consequences your being will have for the world. Sometimes the struggle can get so black, as it did for Jesus on the cross, that we feel that prayer itself is beyond us. But suffering under such inward incapacity to pray is already, in a very deep and real sense, prayer.

Ask. Ask. Ask. Allow your heart to be the theatre of God's engagement with the world around you and before you. Allow God's desires to speak through you.

Of course it does make a difference how we ask. You know that song, "Seek ye first the kingdom of God and his right-eousness. / And all these things shall be added unto you, allelu, alleluia!"? You can't seek first for all these things to be added unto you, and then, as an afterthought, seek the kingdom of God. The principle is somewhat similar to what Augustine was getting at when he said, "Love God and do what you want." If prayer is first of all a relationship with God, then being in that relationship is where the asking starts. We move forward from there as God's companions in building a new world. There is no finding without seeking.

And about those cargo cults. Don't be fooled into thinking that they are as naïve as you have imagined. The cargo desired is a symbol of a new life of dignity and well-being for a dispossessed people who have allowed God's desire to be theirs, to live that out, to build on their hopes for a new and different world, for the kingdom of God. So it has always been with God's people.

Proper 13 C: "Cash in the attic"

Luke 12:13–21

Max Beerbohm, in the 1890s, celebrated the return of women's makeup and all things artificial after the natural, washed faces of the Romantic era. This was in *The Yellow Book*, a periodical dedicated to the aestheticism and decadence of what the French were calling the *fin de siècle*, the years when Liliane Bettencourt's father invented the hair dye that led to *L'Oréal* and the family billions. The *fin de siècle* was the end of the era of Victorian cultural optimism, an era that met its final closure in World War I.

The kind of personal indulgence we see in the parable of the rich man and his overflowing barns, the resolve to 'eat, drink and be merry', finds its natural setting in such moments of history. These are moments that echo the cultural weariness of Ecclesiastes, the literary source of this resolve: "Eat your bread with enjoyment, and drink your wine with a merry heart" (9:7). All is vanity, says the preacher.

The parable tells the story of the last century, the century of Daniel Bell's *The End of Ideology* (1960), describing the collapse of the big ideologies inherited from the nineteenth and early twentieth centuries, the postmodern movement, proclaiming the end of all our "grand narratives", and Francis Fukuyama's *The End of History* (1992), arguing for the end of ideological evolution in the triumph of Western-style liberal democracy. Whatever the intellectual merits of these arguments, they reflect our collective sense that something formerly secure has come to an end. The only remaining certainty seems to be the greed of neo-liberal economics that keeps the markets lumbering in weary cycles of boom and bust. Eat, drink and be merry. All is vanity. We have turned vanity into a creed.

For a while there was a kind of popular apocalypticism that

envisioned not just a collapse of an old order but the advent of something new – an idea popularly proclaimed by Bob Dylan:

> The order is
> Rapidly fadin'
> And the first one now
> Will later be last
> For the times they are a-changin'

This kind of vision arises from a sense of crisis rather than acquiescence, and finds its parallel in the apocalypticism of the Gospels. Jesus, in our story, refuses to take sides in a family money squabble. We will all be judged when death puts an end to indulgence and the pattern of our lives evaporates in smoke, whether personal death or the death of an entire world built on such values. Here the *fin de siècle* is not a collapse into powerless decadence, but an end of indulgence in a victory of what is just and socially engaged.

The Dylan generation's anticipation of a new world dawning largely faded in the 1980s and 90s. A new Max Beerbohm could celebrate the return to glamour and the decadence of self-indulgence in unanticipated intensity. Though a certain wing of the Church would continue to cling to a literal version of the millennial vision of a Second Coming, by and large the former anticipation of a new world has collapsed in an era whose only plot lines seem to be provided by mindless video games. What we once hoped for and worked for has been crowded out by the word of daytime television: *Cash in the Attic, Antiques Roadshow, Homes Under the Hammer*, and so on. Belief in a new future for all has been taken over by belief in the Lottery.

Has the rich man with his big barns won the day, then? Is the apocalyptic vision of a new day reduced to the dark nihilism of *Apocalypse Now*? Of course not. I don't think apocalypticism was ever meant to be taken literally. As a story of crisis, it remains a vital vision for a people of faith in an otherwise vacuous world. The poet Wallace Stevens called this kind of story "supreme fiction" – a story to believe in, decide by and act on. Its truth is validated in faithful action, in commitments arising out of crisis. In a post-religious world, when God seems so silent and the future empty, we must still bravely sing,

> You will see my Jesus come,
> His glory shining like the sun,
> Looking to my Lord's right hand
> When the stars begin to fall.
> My Lord, what a morning!
> My Lord, what a morning!
> Oh, my Lord, what a morning
> When the stars begin to fall.

Proper 14 C: "Don't be afraid"

Luke 12:32–40

Don't be afraid. Get dressed for action. The time has come to decide whether you are going to fish or cut bait. Or, as our Gospel says, "From everyone to whom much has been given, much will be required" (Luke 12:48). There comes a time in the Christian journey, an "Aha!" moment, when it suddenly dawns on us that we are involved in the fulfillment of the promises that have been extended to us.

Faith, according to the anonymous author of Hebrews, anticipates what has been promised, and becomes itself part of the promise.

This is the challenge of living in a godless world, isn't it? We spend years secretly and sometimes openly doubting the existence of a God who never seems to fulfill promises, until it suddenly dawns on us that we – we who have been called to love as we have been loved – it dawns on us that we ourselves are the promise. God is with us. Not out there, but with us as Emmanuel. That is the good news. As Teresa of Avila said, "God has no body, no hands, no feet on earth but ours." The time has come to decide. Are we still disciples, still receiving? Or are we ready to be apostles, ready to give, ready to be sent, to heal, liberate, transform and make things new as God's presence in the world?

The world around us may seem just as forsaken as the impoverished people of Haiti, who in their vulnerability endured decade after decade of exploitation and abuse from European nations, and then came the earthquake. Still today there is rubble, homelessness and not much hope. The story is hardly different from what we find in countless sprawling slums around the world, though Port au Prince has had its fifteen minutes of fame. Tackling the challenges of poverty and corruption, the challenges of drugs and alcoholism and family breakdown, of homophobia and racism and religious extremism, the global challenges of terror and war, debt, economic exploitation, human trafficking, oil dependency and global warming – all this may seem as hopeless as transforming the earthquake rubble of Haiti into a leafy suburban housing development. Can it be done? All we know is that failing to act in the face of such enormous challenges is demonstrating a faith that is, in the words of James the brother of Jesus, truly dead.

Or perhaps failing to act demonstrates not so much a dead faith as a distorted faith, a faith that finds comfort in keeping the world as it is instead of transforming it. The early Christians were recognized as a people who turned the world upside down, a people who refused to settle for what is and through their lives and by their prayers worked for what might be.

What they did by faith became contemporary evidence for a world that was hoped for. These early Christians rejected violence and put the needs of the oppressed and the poor at the center of their corporate life. They lived out the compassion of the cross in a way that turned upside down a world dominated by money and military muscle.

All this changed when in the fourth century Constantine took over Christianity and turned it into the official religion of the Empire. Now the cross was carried into battle as the banner of a culture of violence. As the Anglican writer Ken Leech has said, the cross became twisted into a swastika, into a weapon used to crush one's opponents and maintain the inerrant and invincible authority of empire. A faith that once prayed for God's kingdom to come on earth became a faith focused less threateningly on what happens to you after you die, on creeds and orthodoxies more concerned with questions about the virgin birth and so on than with what Jesus taught about how Christians ought to live. The church's evangelical mission to proclaim the kingdom of God became, instead, a mirror of imperialism, a means of expanding the ecclesiastical franchise. When the Roman Empire co-opted Christianity, it twisted the faith of Jesus Christ into a tool of empire, a faith afraid to question, afraid to challenge, afraid to risk, afraid to hope, afraid to live.

In our Gospel lesson, Jesus says, "Do not be afraid, for it is your Father's good pleasure to give you the kingdom." We are called to be ready for action. If we settle for the way things are, then of all people we are most to be pitied. Our faith is dead. "Where your treasure is, there your heart will be also," Jesus teaches here. If we find our treasure tied up in the way things are now, a state of affairs that causes suffering for many and threatens the future viability of human existence, then of all people we are most to be pitied. Our faith has become twisted and corrupt, and our hearts have become tied to self-preservation, a sad distortion of Christian faith.

Do not be afraid, Jesus says. And he spells out a courageous way of life through which the kingdom may come. It won't be easy. I remember First Presbyterian Church, Chicago, that sits in the middle of what was then a vast, burned out, rubble-strewn slum that seemed the very emblem of communities of devastation everywhere, from Port-au-Prince to Lagos. In a visionary attempt to transform the wasteland around the church, to make the desert bloom, they took delivery of the soil required to make the urban rubble into a fertile garden. What they received was a truckload of toxic, industrial sludge. This is what it is like to live a godly life in a godless world. Somebody is always going to be trying to cash in on your innocence and vulnerability. Don't let it happen. Don't be afraid, Jesus says. Live boldly in a way that anticipates a world that has not yet been seen, and stand firm. When you plant your garden, do not settle for a truckload of toxic, industrial sludge. Complain. Get on the phone to the County Council. Call in the media. Raise hell. That's what First Presbyterian Church, Chicago, did. Make it clear to everyone what God requires. Be an evangelist for the kingdom.

Proper 15 C: "The force that through the green fuse drives the flower"

Hebrews 11.29–12:2; Luke 12.49–56

"I came to cast fire on the earth," Jesus says. If you think I came for peace on earth, you can think again. Jesus came to shatter things in disunity. He came to set family members against one another, son against father and mother against daughter. He came to dethrone the family as the focus of our value system.

Thank goodness this reading is hidden away in August when everyone is on holiday. This is just not going to cut it as a lesson to be read at Christmas, when family harmony must be achieved at all cost. Peace on earth, indeed.

When the feast of Christ's nativity does come, should we bury this in the back of the closet, hide it away, forget it, so that we can have a good Christmas? Remember that just after all those cute little Christmas play stories about shepherds and angels and "peace on earth" and all that, Simeon tells the mother of the newborn infant that this child has come for the destruction and salvation of many, that many will rise up against him, and that he will cause Mary sorrow that will pierce her heart like a sharp sword. Christmas is no stranger to conflict.

Hugh Halverstadt, in *Managing Church Conflict*, reminds us that there is good conflict and bad conflict. There is tension that is creative and renewing and there is tension that is corrosive and malignant. We need to be courageous enough to embrace the former and courageous enough to stand against the latter.

The biblical concept of Torah, of law, for instance, represents a deep order and fecundity at the heart of all things that is full of dynamism and tension. Torah is not about conformity but liberation for life together, life coming to be, the courageous integrity of the smallest things. It's the Moses story, and how the struggles of the Moses story illustrate something fundamental about life.

You will recognize that the title of this meditation for Proper 15 C comes from a poem by the Welsh poet Dylan Thomas. The poem celebrates the kind of dynamism and tension we share with all things that are. "The force that through the green fuse drives the flower," Thomas says, "drives my green age." This is the dynamism of death as well as life. All is alive, even death. What "blasts the roots of trees," he says, is also "my destroyer." His youth, he says, is "bent by the same wintry fever" as "the crooked rose."

The same energy running through living nature runs through human life. "The force that drives the water through the rocks," he says, is the same force that drives his red blood.

Life is dynamic, pulsing with tension and force. We who are born, fall in love, flourish for a while and die are part of that dynamism. What happens in my veins is what happens in mountain springs.

So when Jesus says he has come to bring the dynamism of tension and conflict to the earth, he is testifying to a creative energy required by any life that has any integrity at all, any courage of its own being. He himself feels this inner tension, he says. He has a baptism to be baptized with, he says, an hour when his life will be perfectly aligned with God's agenda. That's what baptism means, isn't it? And he tells us how he is stretched by an inner tension for this to be accomplished. The Authorized Version says he is "straightened", stretched out, taut, tense.

The Letter to the Hebrews seems to be saying that faith is not a matter of belief in God but belief in God's agenda for you and for the world. That is the root of desire that burned in the heart of Jesus, that stretched the sinews of his soul and made him come alive as the Son of God. That is the creative tension we all need to be stretched by. The Bible, as it discloses God's agenda, needs to be a kind of WikiLeaks for us, to enable us to see, clearly and courageously, what is really going on in our lives and in our world, despite the disharmony that might result among all those whose lives are bound up with the petty competing claims for absolute loyalties around us.

They say Dylan Thomas is not well remembered in the area of Wales he comes from. He'd left behind a string of bad debts, broken relationships and unresolved arguments. This only represents the kind of conflict arising naturally from the soul of someone at odds with sleepy bourgeois normalcy, I submit. We can recall Kierkegaard's critique of 'Christendom' as a covert transformation of Christian discipleship into a bourgeois way of life (autonomy, property, stability, success). The memories Thomas left behind had to do with the tensions of a creative spirit. You can't write poetry without it. You can write sentimental greeting card verse, but you can't write poetry. Today, however, now that the West Wales of his roots have recognized the tourist potential of his reputation, all is at peace, the kind of peace that for the sake of profit kills the prophet.

It is no secret that the pressures of neighborhoods, families, class expectations and often religion itself can crush a person to the point where his or her life becomes chaotic, dysfunctional and sometimes even violent. If you want to discover the roots of anti-social behavior, just visit some of our primary schools where you can still hear teachers shouting at students many years after they buried the cane. You could even say that the pressure to keep the peace, to live life undisturbed and non-conflictual is the pressure that casts so many people out into a life that becomes a longing, lonely prayer to count for something in a world that has, for them, become a nightmare.

For Jesus, the courage to abandon his own peace in order to enter into the lack of peace experienced by others was what the incarnation was all about. Catholic theologian Johann Baptist Metz calls this "that militant love that draws upon itself the suffering of others." Entering into the world of others' pain, we find the genuine godly peace of God's loving engagement with the world.

St. Augustine said that Christ is present with people not so much in moments of peace that look like those tranquil calendar-art landscapes. Christ becomes present in moments of "severe trial," he says, and he goes on to say that "we progress by means of trial... No one knows himself except through trial." The cross we take up in faith becomes the means of a self-discovery that is also a discovery of God's agenda for the world.

Proper 16 C: "The bent-over woman"

Luke 13:10–17

They've invented mattresses for cows. An agricultural products company in Northern Ireland has marketed Pasture Mats and Poly Pillows, which are like beanbags covered by army blankets and filled with rubber crumbs from old car tires. The theory is that happy cows produce more milk.

The news reminds me of the slogan for a certain brand of condensed milk which in my youth was advertised as having come from "contented cows." The image of contented cows grazing in lazy green pastures on warm, sunny days and reclining on their Pasture Mats at night seems to me a terrific image of Sabbath rest, and reminds me of the stress-free Sundays I grew up with – no dishes to wash, no shopping to do, no lawns to mow, no floors to polish, no cars to wash. Sunday was Sunday, a day of contentment, a day of rest.

Only my mother was exempt from such Sabbath indolence, as, in the post-war absence of live-in help, she had to prepare our Sunday lunch.

In Luke 13 Jesus liberates a woman from eighteen years of living bent over, a woman who is the very emblem of gender-based oppression, and in doing so he illuminates what Sabbath rest is all about. "Remember that you were a slave in the land of Egypt," we read in the Ten Commandments, "and the Lord your God brought you out from there with a mighty hand and an outstretched arm. Therefore (!) the Lord your God commanded you to keep the Sabbath day." Sabbath rest is a declaration that we are not made to be bent-over beasts of burden. We are meant to stand up as free people. The command to remember the Sabbath always has this social, political meaning in the background.

Isaiah puts it very clearly. He says (58:9) you are honoring the

Sabbath if you remove the yoke of oppression from among you. You are giving honor to the Sabbath and you are going to shine like the sun in the kingdom of heaven.

On the other hand, if you seek to promote your own interests at the expense of others, you are trampling the Sabbath into the dust.

To make Sunday special, as the campaign against Sunday opening hours used to say, is not a matter of not shopping on Sunday. It is, more positively, a matter of doing justice.

Look what happens here. Jesus is teaching in the synagogue on the Sabbath. Imagine what he might be teaching – more than likely his pet theme – we all have pet themes – I've preached the same sermon for over thirty years – Jesus is teaching his pet theme, the good news of the kingdom of God, the kind of thing he has been hammering on about since the very beginning of his ministry, liberation for the captives, good news for the poor, the kind of society in which burdens are lifted. This woman comes in, bent over, a living metaphor for everything he has been saying, and he turns to her and declares to her that she is free from what has been oppressing her all these long years.

The leader of the synagogue doesn't get it. He thinks the Sabbath is all about prohibitions. The leader of the synagogue doesn't recognize that Jesus has invoked the fundamental meaning of Sabbath rest as it is grounded in the memory of Exodus freedom from slavery and the promise of liberation in kingdom come.

All the leader of the synagogue sees is the thin literal surface of what's happened, an act of healing. Healing is his term, not how Jesus sees it. It is as if we were only speaking of overcoming something like osteoporosis here without this deep resonance of meaning the tradition of the Sabbath has had for the Jewish people. The leader of the synagogue has forgotten what we are here for. Isn't it funny how the church, concerned only for its own survival, so often forgets what it's here for? Or maybe "funny" isn't the world I'm looking for.

Notice how this local leader has begun to panic. His whole life has been dedicated to keeping this institution running, well-oiled and filling the needs of the community. And now this Jesus in one irreverent act is causing everything to fall apart. He turns to the gathered crowd – visualize this! – and he says, in a loud voice, "There are six days to work. You can come for healing all week long, but don't come for healing on the Sabbath!" Notice how the story says he keeps repeating this, over and over, desperately trying to limit the damage by deflecting attention away from Jesus.

In answering him, Jesus speaks to the crowd. He calls them hypocrites. A hypocrite is someone who goes through the motions of practicing a faithful religious life but actually hasn't a clue what it is really all about. The Sabbath is about the liberation of the sons and daughters of Abraham, and shouldn't this woman, who has been bound all these years, be set free? It's not a question of waiting until tomorrow. Such liberty is what the Sabbath is all about.

Our story from Luke 13 is perhaps chiefly concerned with bent-over women, and with the status of women in a church that has traditionally been dominated by men. Amnesty International, for instance, in a long- and carefully-considered position on abortion rights for women who have suffered from the violence of conflict and war in which rape has been used as a political weapon, experienced heated international opposition from the Catholic Church. "From the battlefield to the bedroom," Amnesty says, "women are at risk." Time and again the Asylum Justice program at City United Reformed Church meets women who have fled violence against them that is not only family but state sanctioned, but their appeal for sanctuary fails because their grounds, as women, are not considered legitimate under the Geneva Convention.

Add to this the way women's bodies are bent through sexed

up clothing, perfumes, anorexia, obsessive forms of dieting and the social passion for cosmetic surgery – facelifts, body contouring, laser skin resurfacing and breast augmentation, reduction or lift. Here's what an advertisement for perfume in a department store window says:

> You want it. You want it bad. Sometimes so much it hurts. You can taste it. You feel like you would do anything to get it. Go further than they'd suspect. Twist your soul and crush what's in your way. Then you get it. And something happens. You become the object of your desire. And it feels incredible.

Curiously, so much of what the world calls standing up for ourselves only increases the angle at which we are so painfully bent over, twisted, our horizons diminished by the perspective of the marketplace and the boxes other people put us in. Sabbath rest liberates us from all this. Or could, if we let it.

Proper 17 C: "The same forever"

Hebrews 13:1–8, 15–16; Luke 14:1, 7–14

There was a sense of permanence and rightness that characterized the rural village world of my early years. Harvests brought the familiar smell of corn dust to my nostrils and the juice of freshly pressed apples. The soft, first snows of winter always seemed to come at night, falling ever slowly and lightly and illuminated in the darkness by the street lamps. Later, in the bitter cold of January, the snow was harder and crunched under our feet as we returned to school after Christmas. Spring came with unruly green, wet wind, color and a packed church on Easter Sunday. And finally there was the sweaty heat and the thistles and the fireflies of summer. The rhythm was the eternally turning rhythm of permanence, like the eternal turning of the lectionary cycle and the never-changing Apostles Creed, recited generation upon generation in timeless, boundless faithfulness. John Updike once described that creed as like "a path worn smooth over the rough terrain of our hearts."

Collapse: How Societies Choose to Fail or Survive, by Jared Diamond, tells the story of cultures like Easter Island that shared such an attachment to permanence and security. Diamond argues that their confidence in permanence was a major factor in their collapse. They were unable to make the extraordinarily difficult and courageous decisions to change the way they were doing things before crisis hit. The time to act was when problems became perceptible, but it didn't happen. Their experience serves as a parable for all who put their confidence in permanence.

Why couldn't they act? Human nature. The rich, the powerful who controlled the resources didn't think the signs of collapse would affect them. We can imagine them singing songs celebrating the never-changing stability of a benevolent world like the ones we used to sing:

The rich man in his castle,
The poor man at his gate,
He made them, high or lowly,
And ordered their estate.
All things bright and beautiful,
All creatures great and small,
All things wise and wonderful:
The Lord God made them all.

The richer classes in these societies thought they could buy themselves the privilege to be the last to starve or the last to die, but this kind of thinking doesn't really gain you ultimate security, and certainly not much security for your children. As long as the hard choices required by the long-term thinking of a society as a whole are avoided, the more that society's collapse is likely.

In Luke 14 we get a critique of the kind of attitudes that cause social collapse. Here, the security of a never-changing world is represented by the social hierarchy of table fellowship, the rich at the head table, the poor sitting back by the clatter of the kitchen. The dining arrangements become a kind of anthropological metaphor for the way those who can manage it always sit in the best places, consume the most stuff and grab the bulk of the resources, like the City fat cats who get 37% pay rises (not to mention bonuses) while prison wardens have to be satisfied with under 2%.

Jesus chooses to sit with the less privileged, here at table and later in the company of condemned thieves. And he never wavers in this choice. This is the kind of stability that can sustain societies and give life to coming generations. Hebrews 13:8 says, "Jesus Christ is the same yesterday, today and forever." With Jesus as the pioneer and perfecter of our faith, we live as he did for the most vulnerable and for generations yet unborn. We do not live as those determined to be the last to starve or the last to die.

The parallels with today's world are obvious. The significant difference is that today we are not talking about isolated, self-contained communities like Easter Island that suffer the consequences of their inability to take the long view and make the hard choices. Today the planet as a whole is as self-contained and isolated as Easter Island was when Western explorers discovered its already collapsed culture in the early eighteenth century.

We live inescapably in a global neighborhood. The highest blood levels of toxic industrial chemicals and pesticides reported for any people in the world are found in the blood of Eskimos living on the remote ice of eastern Greenland and Siberia, about as far away as you can get from the places where they use this kind of stuff.

One of the world's most remote bits of land is a small, isolated, uninhabited atoll in the South Pacific, a hundred miles from its nearest island neighbor, also uninhabited. The beaches of this remote speck of land are littered with garbage, plastic bags, buoys, glass and plastic bottles, rope, shoes, light bulbs, footballs, plastic toy soldiers and airplanes, bike peddles, screwdrivers and so on.

And then there is the more familiar story of an atmosphere polluted by an increasingly urban and increasingly energy-hungry expanding population. Invisible, out of sight and often out of mind, the 800 gigatons of carbon in the atmosphere represent a 70% increase in the concentration of carbon dioxide in the last fifty years alone. We are all in this together, willy-nilly.

Is there hope? What Jesus gives us is really so very, very simple – an abundant life illustrated by this simple gesture of taking a seat among the humble. There we find the fundamental virtues of mutual love, hospitality, concern for the imprisoned, the refugee, the trafficked, the victims of torture, the virtue of loyalty and commitment to the stranger, and selfless resistance to a life ruled by money. That's what Jesus is always all about. It's courageous. It's revolutionary. It's a permanent revolution. And you can count on it, because this is what Jesus has been about from before time began, is what Jesus is about whenever we break bread together today, and will be what Jesus is about when this planet earth falls back into the sun from which it came.

Proper 18 C: "Invitation to choose"

Deuteronomy 30:15–20; Luke 14:25–33

On 29 September in 1904, more than a hundred years ago, at a revival meeting organized by Joseph Jenkins, Seth Joshua called out a plea to God: "Humble me, O Lord," he cried.

Then Evan Roberts, famously, fell like a stone with his arms draped over the seat in front of him. "Humble me... humble me... humble me..." he called.

One of the electrifying things that happened in the revival services held over the following twelve months was the repetition among the congregation of a short phrase like this or a sentence, like "Send the Spirit down, O Lord," and this would be taken up by one and then another until it was being chanted by the entire assembly, and the fire of the Holy Spirit would fall.

Now imagine a similar scene – a gathering of believers and would-be-believers in ancient Israel. Imagine this gathering taking place at a time of institutional and social decline, the faith that had brought this people out of the shackles of Egyptian slavery was being compromised by the new affluence of Israel's leaders, by the growing gap between rich and poor, and by the insidious influences of foreign cultures – blue jeans, rock and roll, women's rights and so on.

Imagine the priest standing before this crowd reading the words of Deuteronomy 30: "I set before you life and death, blessing and curse, good and evil. I set before you life and death. For God's sake, choose life, that you and your descendants may live."

And then he echoes what he has just said, marking out each word with its own emphasis: "WE – WILL – CHOOSE – LIFE."

And then someone else out in the crowd calls out the same words: "WE – WILL – CHOOSE – LIFE!" And then another and another, and another: "WE – WILL –CHOOSE – LIFE!" until the assembly is thundering with equal enthusiasm. "WE – WILL – CHOOSE – LIFE!"

As in the Welsh Revival of 1904, this is a highly charged moment. It is a time for renewal of commitment.

And as in the Welsh Revival of 1904, there would be disruptions in families and among neighbors as the intensity pervaded every corner of life, just as Jesus said would happen for those disciples willing to pay the cost of their discipleship. It was a collective fervor of shared conviction that enabled people's lives to change.

And so it happened in 1904. Real changes came in people's lives. No more alcohol, no more violence, no more running around at night and no more gambling. Those touched by the revival became aware of the cost of discipleship, and paid it. Lives changed. Break times down in the mines became prayer meetings.

The big question so many are asking now is whether such revival is viable today. Anglican theologian DR Davies, an ex-Congregationalist minister who had begun his own preaching under the influence of the Welsh Revival, has said in his autobiography that the revival was the swan song of an old-time religion. It was the consumptive flush of death that gives the appearance of revival in a tradition that belonged essentially to the past.

American church historian Martin Marty once observed that similar revivals sweeping through my home country like Midwestern summer thunderstorms always left the Church worse off afterward than it had been before. And William May, in *Testing the National Covenant*, reminds us that in the ebb and flow of church life in the period before 1860 that experienced three great waves of these revivals, institutional religion generally ebbed more than it flowed. These were, in any case, the churches that trace their heritage to the Reformation, like mine. Today we might take a different, more global perspective. Stephen

Prothero, in *God Is Not One: The Eight Rival Religions That Run the World – and Why Their Differences Matter*, says churches flying the flag of the Reformation had their last heyday in the eighteenth century, but were already looking like an endangered species then. The nineteenth century was the century of the Evangelicals. The twentieth century belonged to the Pentecostals. Philip Jenkins, in *The Next Christendom: The Coming of Global Christianity*, shows how Christianity is growing at a phenomenal rate in the Southern hemisphere and in China, while the West, engrossed in tolerance and affluence, sees its Christianity in decline. The Pentecostal, charismatic and indigenous religion-influenced churches of the South that are emerging as today's main players may look unrecognizable to us as Christianity, but this is the next Christendom. And there is something about its flourishing that reaches back to the original heart of Christianity, says Jenkins. Christianity grows among the poor and persecuted. It atrophies among the rich and secure.

Nevertheless, from where we sit, from the perspective of the Old Christendom, a critical question faces us. Can our contemporary world afford religious fervor of any kind? Jesus says, "Whoever comes to me and does not hate father and mother, wife and children, brothers and sisters, yes, and even life itself, cannot be my disciple." As we look at the questions raised by this reading from Luke 14, about the religious commitment of true believers, about self-sacrificial devotion to a cause, about making hard choices between issues that have taken on a black-and-white intensity, we must do so in the presence of, for instance, the violence of the Boko Haram sect in Nigeria and in the light of the radical self-sacrificial, bomb-clad faith of the al-Qaida movement. Can the world still afford religiously-driven passion?

In the aftermath of the Holocaust, Irving Greenberg said that, from now on, "no statement, theological or otherwise, should be made that could not be credible in the presence of burning children."

Perhaps we should all become lukewarm, blancmange Western post-Christendom liberals condemning radical intensity out of hand. This puts us in the territory of that line from Yeats' "The Second Coming": "The best lack all conviction, while the worst / Are full of passionate intensity."

The answer Jesus gives to both the wishy-washy Western liberals and the impassioned Christians of the South is the cross. "Whoever does not carry the cross and follow me cannot be my disciple" (Luke 14:27). The cross of Jesus is the proclamation of shared suffering, of a shared suffering that can transform our twenty-first century global battleground into something like table fellowship. Don't let the cross be hijacked by the jewelry industry or by those who would use it as an emblem of success or expansionist zeal. When we choose, this cross of shared suffering is the only cross we have to choose. It is the cross that affirms life together in the very grip of death. Choose life.

If by some wild chance there is to be a new revival in Wales today, which, to be honest, I doubt and sometimes actually dread, anticipating the form it would take, I would hope that its foundation might be this difficult decision to live in the cruciform intersection of all humanity, where Jesus chose to live, taking on one another's brokenness as our own, that in our shared brokenness we might discover the healing of the nations.

Proper 19 C: "Hard-wired care"

Luke 15:1–10

There is something deep in the human spirit that panics when something is lost and rejoices when something is found – things like keys, spectacles, bus passes, or sons, or, as the case may be, daughters.

Daughters or sons who finally come back home after a God-only-knows-where absence expect all hell to break loose in a torrent of angry judgment. They become disoriented by their parents' overwhelming sense of relief and joy at their safe homecoming. Jesus says this is just basic humanity. "Which one of you," he says, verse 4, "having a hundred sheep and losing one of them, does not leave the ninety-nine in the wilderness and go after the one that is lost until he finds it?" This is the way we are. And he says God is like this, too. The philosopher Alfred North Whitehead once described God as "a tender care that nothing be lost."

I would imagine that when the slave trade was abolished and ultimately slavery itself was abolished there was a sense of joy among the abolitionists that a people once lost had been found. A fundamental humanity had been lost, not only the fundamental humanity of the slaves but also the fundamental humanity of those who bought them and sold them and used their labor to feed Britain's Industrial Revolution.

The massive scale of the slave trade can only be understood in the context of that unprecedented, voracious appetite of the mills for cotton. And it wasn't just the slaves and their traders who were stripped of their humanity by this economic jungle. The victims of Britain's industrialization also included child laborers who worked 18 hour shifts and were maimed and sometimes actually pulled in and cut to bits by the machines they worked at. The managers' duty to profit would not allow them to shut down production long enough to rescue such a child. I want to use this image of the machinery of the Industrial Revolution and the way it drove a depersonalized system as a metaphor for a depersonalizing world in which people become lost.

Human beings became dehumanized pieces of the new machinery and the increasingly global markets for agricultural goods and manufactured products. And then, with the abolition of slavery, people gradually began to sense what it meant to be found again as living, vital, enfleshed human beings. In 1779 John Newton, the slave trader, said, "I once was lost, but now am found." A whole generation of people, black and white together, could sing the same song at last.

But of course we remain lost, alienated, cogs in machinery and systems that still dehumanize us. When I was an undergraduate we studied psychology by training rats to run through mazes with rewards that are no different at all from the incentives calculated to drive us through the rat races of the twenty-first century. Urban sociologist Richard Sennett describes contemporary management practices as particularly dehumanizing. They corrupt our character, he says, damage families and tear apart the fabric of communities. The machinery today may be less mechanical and more electronic, but the process of dehumanization is just as virulent, and an increasingly globalized market creates a hunger for migrant labor and trafficked humanity and manufacturing outsourced to wherever people are forced to work for a pat on the back. Maybe there is not much difference from the days of slavery after all. And it is not just slaves who have lost their humanity. We who profit from their labor have lost our humanity as well, just as in the eighteenth century.

In a sense, there is no more humanity. Our souls have been reduced to the data computers yield from their analysis of the numbers from our bank cards and loyalty cards. We think we choose, but the marketing people have our profiles down so accurately that we buy what they want us to buy. John Kenneth

Galbraith, in *The Economics of Innocent Fraud*, says, "Belief in a market economy in which the consumer is sovereign is one of our most pervasive forms of fraud." "Corporate power," he says,

> ... has shaped the public purpose to its own ability and need. It ordains that social success is more automobiles, more television sets, more diverse apparel, a greater volume of all other consumer goods. Also more and more lethal weapons. Here is the measure of human achievement. Negative social effects – pollution, destruction of the landscape, the unprotected health of the citizenry, the threat of military action and death – do not count as such.

We say we are free, we even say we export freedom and democracy to places like Iraq, but what is produced is deeper mayhem and violence, and the cynicism of our promise of freedom becomes exposed as Iraqi oil reserves become devoured by British and American firms. Our good life requires the suffering of many. The world knows this. We don't. We need a new kind of William Wilberforce to open our minds to the world we live in. We need to be in Christ, for in Christ, as Paul says, there is a new creation. Our need is that radical, and it is a need that must be pressed hard in every generation.

For the first four hundred years of its history the pictorial imagery of Christianity – wall paintings, mosaics, etc. – drew on pagan sources, with Christ depicted as Apollo or Orpheus. The most popular image of Christ was a Hermes-like picture of a shepherd carrying a lamb across his shoulders, the lost lamb of the story. The cross and the crucifix came many years later and did not really become conventional iconography until the eighth century. Before that it was the shepherd rejoicing at finding the lost lamb, and bringing it home.

We would do well to recover this tender humanity of the early church. People were just as lost then as now, lost in the political, economic worlds they struggled to live in and even in the world of their faith. Peasants labored, gripped in the iron fist of the Roman Empire, in one of the most unjust agricultural economies we have known, with double taxation and insecure tenant farming growing as more and more land fell into the hands of absentee landowners. In the world of faith, ritual purity laws dehumanized people with labels of uncleanliness, temple-based hierarchies pushed God further and further away from human experience.

In a tender manner, Jesus simply embraced people, affirmed them, touched them, overcame stigma and exclusion, so mediating to them the grace of God and so restoring their humanity. Those who had been lost were found, and there was great joy and great feasting. In the northern European form of Christianity we have inherited, dark, penitential and privatized, we have forgotten such gladness.

In its pre-Christian setting, the image of a lamb carried over the shoulders was an image of being carried into an afterlife. It was an image of a new dawn that comes as the Good Shepherd recovers what is lost, an image of fundamental hope in the hearts of those who have been betrayed and abandoned to the dehumanizing systems of the world. The hope is that a tender care for what has been lost truly does belong to what is divine. Jesus said, "Yes, this is what God is like."

But then he went beyond that savage pagan world in which people lived so dependently on their gods. He said this is a tender care that is also hard wired into what it means to be human. "Who among you," he says to the Pharisees, "wouldn't go searching for what is lost?" Jesus is not just telling us something about God, or about himself, but about us, and the way we are called to live as a church and as disciples. Think of the people even among those we know who are dehumanized by prejudice, by labels, stereotypes and statistics, bar codes and data banks, people who have become lost in a tide of forces beyond them. Can we reach out and touch them as Jesus did, in ways that restore our humanity? Isn't this what Paul means when he asks us to be ambassadors for Christ? And then, as a church, can we learn to feast when we have found one another?

Proper 20 C: "Side by Side"

Amos 8:4–7; Luke 16:1–13

The parable is about money and since the parable is addressed to the cardboard caricature Pharisees, who love money as much as they resent the ne'er-do-wells Jesus invites to his table, the parable implies that religious people can get their priorities screwed up.

Religious people can take fiscal responsibility more seriously than they do the call to love as extravagantly as Jesus did. Being foolish with money becomes the greatest sin. The prophet Amos, in the Old Testament, puts it even more harshly. He says we can hardly wait for this Sunday service to end before we get back to the business of getting rich by gouging the poor.

But the parable doesn't start out that way. The parable starts out where we are, as people concerned for the proper management of money.

The rich man in the parable is fulminating against the irresponsible management of his accounts. He could just as well be fulminating against the irresponsible lending, the aggressive marketing of easy credit and the over-extended budgets that led to a global economic collapse that seems to know no end. And he shouldn't just be fulminating against the directors of particular banks or absent-minded government regulators, but against the culture we live in, breathe and ingest. We are as outraged as the rich man in the parable. Our money simply ought to be managed better. Failing, state-owned banks continue to give millions in bonuses. And the Pharisees who are listening to this story agree, for they love money, says the Gospel, verse 14. Financial mismanagement and economic collapse go hand in hand, then as now.

So the rich man in the parable tells his manager to hand in his account. He's fired. And this means the manager is really sunk. What is he going to do now? he thinks. Management is the only thing he knows how to do. He sits behind a desk all day long, so he won't be any good for manual labor. And he is too proud to go on the dole. What is he going to do?

He thinks through his options as the Prodigal Son had in the other story, and he hits on a brilliant survival scheme. He still has his master's account books. He goes around to all his master's creditors and cuts deals with them to ensure that he has plenty of friends who will welcome him when he gets canned.

He slashes what they owe, taking twenty percent off one, fifty percent off another. He's making friends at the boss's expense, as if he is working for the Jubilee 2000 debt relief campaign.

Can you imagine how the boss is going to react when his manager presents him with these accounts? Could you imagine the rage that the Prodigal Son thought he would meet when he came home to tell his father that he had wasted half the family's fortune on a weekend of debauchery? But it didn't happen then. And it doesn't happen now. The expectation we all have for a just judgment against this crook is frustrated. It doesn't happen. The boss commends him for his shrewdness. It's crazy, isn't it?

The Pharisees, who love money, sneer at Jesus when he tells this story. The parable has not turned out to be the kind of harsh story of judgment we anticipated, the kind you might find in the Gospel of Matthew. Here in Luke the irresponsible manager is not kicked out into the outer darkness where he will weep and gnash his teeth because he has (horrors!) committed the terrible sin of mismanaging *money*. On the contrary, the manager's ingenious but fiscally irresponsible solution to his problem actually delights the boss. This is entirely unexpected and an affront to our sensibilities. The Pharisees sneer at Jesus when they hear this story, literally turn up their noses in contempt.

There are alternatives to a culture driven by money. When I was a young kid in the lean post-war years of the early 1950s we used to enjoy singing that *Side by Side* song:

Well we ain't got a barrel of money...
We may look ragged and funny...
But we're travelin' on...
Singin' our song...
Side by side.

"What if the sky should fall?" the song continues. "As long as we're together, / It doesn't matter at all." I remember Ronnie Corbett saying he and his wife were so poor in those days that they were grateful when their landlord invited them downstairs to dip their toast in his egg. There was no particular virtue in that way of life. But our lives were not driven by money.

"As long as we're together" is the Gospel message that is so much more important than money. Some of you can remember stories from those lean years before the economic get-rich years of the 1960s and 70s and 80s and 90s and the early years of the new millennium.

We need to remember that our religious faith is not an optimism that everything is going to turn out all right. Faith is discipleship. Faith is my confidence that the life Jesus lived is the proper shape of my own life. Jesus, for the sake of others, became poor.

Faith is a concern for the life of my neighbor that is strong enough to enable me to put anxieties for my own security to one side. Faith enables me to cut back on what I spend on myself because I am determined for things to go well not just with me but with you and particularly with those who are now in need. My faith is the shape of my life and the choices I make.

This is how God provides. God provides when the people of God are compassionate as God is compassionate (Luke 6:36). The way the faithful deliberately plan their budgets to be able to share what they have with others is what the Bible means by God providing. And more topically, the Jubilee campaign for debt relief is part of God's providence (see Leviticus 25). The Pharisees of this world just can't understand this. They sneer at the naïveté of those who take compassion so seriously. Well, let them, is what I say. As long as we're together, it doesn't matter at all.

Proper 21 C: "Holding hands"

Luke 16:19–31

In the days of slavery in my home country African Americans sang an exuberant hope for a better life to come. One of their songs went like this:

I got shoes you got shoes
all of God's childrens got shoes
When I get to heaven gonna put on my shoes
I'm gonna walk all over God's heaven
(heaven) heaven (heaven)
Everybody talkin' bout heaven ain't a goin' there
heaven (heaven) heaven (heaven)

The song gained its poignancy from the reality that those who sang it had no shoes. Heaven was a better world where they would have shoes like everyone else. Heaven was going to be a place of basic dignity, justice, and affirmation for those now downtrodden. They would put on their shoes and walk all over, with all the delight you could already hear in this song of anticipation.

In the days of the Civil Rights Movement those of us who had never sung this song were taught that it was not just a pie-in-the-sky dream. It had in it an aspiration for a changed world where all God's children would indeed wear shoes, the kind of world we pray for in the Lord's Prayer: "Thy will be done on earth." "As they accepted the promise and took it to themselves," says James Cone in *The Spirituals and the Blues*, "it became a real force in their history; hence 'a new dimension of promise and new reality.' The promise of heaven in black music placed the people in a 'New Earth' and transformed their perceptions of black existence from the nothingness of the present condition of slavery into being-for-future." One day we will all wear shoes regardless of our skin color.

Our story in Luke 16 tells of a poor man named Lazarus. His name means "God is my help" – God helps when no one else is helping. He's about as poor as you can get. A beggar, lying at the gate of a rich man's house, covered in sores, hungry, desperate. Lazarus is like the slave, with no one to help him but God. His only hope is in heaven. The story is the story of a world that has found no room for compassion, where the only succor for the destitute is their hope for heaven.

The story of the rich man and Lazarus has all the markings of a popular folk tale, with the popular view of an afterlife in which people go to their just rewards, some to Abraham's bosom and some to eternal torment. Stories like this were as popular in the day of Jesus as the jokes today about what happens to people when they die and go to meet St. Peter at the gates of Heaven. Will they get in or not? What will it be like? At the end of the day the comic reversal in these St. Peter stories is always about life here and now.

The young people at City United Reformed Church acted out this parable at our Harvest Festival. The way the young lad playing the rich man bragged gloriously about his wealth was mirrored in our ostentatious harvest display of garden vegetables that looked like they had all won first prize at the county agricultural fair. The marrows and the cabbages and the mounds of apples were joined by large sacks of potatoes and sacks of rice and standing stalks of sweet corn. The way they played it emphasized the way the good life we were celebrating at Harvest distracts us from those like Lazarus who lie hungry and in misery at the gate of the Church. It was poignant and even painful. This is what young people like to do. They like to embarrass the church. You give them free rein to be creative and they stick it to you every time.

At the end of the play angels dressed in white have carried

the dead Lazarus up into the pulpit to be with Abraham. One of the older girls, all in black, has carried the rich man's body off to the side, by the choir.

I remember attending a funeral once in my youth. One of our classmates had been struck by lightning. I'll never forget how the preacher, after giving cursory attention to our friend's life, said that it was too late now for Jimmy. But it wasn't too late for us, and he proceeded to hold out the prospect of a vividly-imagined hellfire that awaited the unwary, and he exhorted us to straighten up and start flying right.

The rich man realizes it is too late for him. So he asks if Lazarus can be sent back from the dead to warn his brothers. What's the point, Abraham asks from the pulpit. If they never paid any attention to Moses, why would they listen to someone who has come back from the dead?

The problem is more biting that we might think. We even blind ourselves to what Moses has to say, despite our faithful churchgoing. John Hull has written a book called *What Prevents Christian Adults from Learning?* Hull says almost all the things we do as churchgoers are ways of avoiding learning.

Opportunities for learning what Christianity means as a way of life that is concerned for others are lost as we focus instead on our declining institutions, keeping the machinery well-oiled, smoothly running from one harvest festival to the next. 'Faith' seems to be a nervous need for assurance that we will never have to change. I remember the first worship service I presided at here in Wales. For the charge and benediction, I invited them to hold hands with one another, as we always did at St. James in Chicago. After the service one of the elders took me aside to tell me, quietly, that British people didn't do such things. Was my invitation to hold hands cultural intrusion, or a failed attempt to introduce a warmer, richer community?

When we meet, conversation floats on the surface of friendship and family. We give praise for those we call 'good workers', those who never fail to show up to fulfill their duty, bake pies and run the PA system. Few dare ever mention generosity, compassion, or dedication to the cause of the destitute, few ever dare speak of their vision for a new and just society in which we ourselves might have to change the way we live, give more, care more in ways that demand changes in the way we spend our money. Lazarus lies at our gate, unremarked.

It is amazing how our lives are dominated by the need to be distracted from what might challenge us. There was a song on the radio when I was a kid that borrowed from that African American song about shoes:

> I got shoes, you got shoes,
> all God's children got shoes.
> But there's only one kind of shoes to buy:
> that's good old Buster Brown shoes!

We don't just go to church to get distracted from the world. The commercial pressure that drives our lives seems to overtake every sentiment of compassionate engagement. The way we unthinkingly live as consumers smothers our ability to see and to learn what is going on in the world around us. The bare-footed Lazarus lies unnoticed at the gate.

On that Harvest Sunday when the youth group did the play, Liz Meek led us in prayer. She based the theme of her prayers on this parable, and challenged us to overcome our blindness and open our eyes to the real distance between us and Lazarus as he still exists in the life of the world around us. Bringing her point home, she invited us to practice overcoming the distance that separates us by holding hands during the prayers – a distinctly *un*-British practice, she acknowledged. She assured us she realized how difficult this would be for us. She promised to keep her prayers short, but this, she suggested, could be a small start on the way to bridging the chasm that divides us.

And when you think about it, though even this would be painful for some, her invitation was the same invitation we get from the resurrected one. It is an invitation into a way of life that in the end is filled with joy and deeper companionship than life lived for ourselves alone can ever be, and filled with far more abundance than any harvest festival can ever imagine.

Proper 22 C: "Come, ye disconsolate"

Lamentations 1:1–6; Luke 17:5–10

Jerusalem "weeps bitterly in the night, with tears on her cheeks; among all her lovers she has no one to comfort her," we read in Lamentations.

I visited a church in Chicago once that had the title of the hymn *Come, Ye Disconsolate* written in big letters across the round arch framing its front door. Al Bridges, who was among the small company of clergy that had gathered to meet there, told the rest of us that Roberta Flack had recently recorded an emotionally powerful rendition of this hymn. "Come, ye disconsolate," she sang in a slow, bluesy, soulful manner. "Here bring your wounded hearts."

Jerusalem's temple and its towers have been razed to the ground, to rubble. Jerusalem's people have been carried off to exile in Babylon, in what today is named Iraq.

Give us confidence in God, the disciples say. "Increase our faith," they ask Jesus. The consolation Jesus gives is to remind them that faith is a matter of discipleship, that faith is found in being faithful. We are like servants, or slaves, Jesus says, only doing our duty. And he gives an example. Say the master is coming in from a long day working in the fields. The slave should not expect to sit down at table with the master. It is the slave's duty to put on an apron and serve. Faith is like this. It is simply doing as we ought.

Marieke tells me this is not a very feminist story. It's a story that reminds her of the fellow who was telling his young son about the day he married the boy's mother, and the boy asks, "Was that the time Mummy came to work for us?"

The image of the slave in the story Jesus tells is not meant to be appealing or to justify any particular social convention. It is meant to be a put-down of all those who ask for a bigger faith when they ought to be asking for bigger discipleship. The slave should not even expect thanks and certainly should not expect glory for simply doing what has been commanded. This is just a matter of duty.

Bob Dylan celebrates such an idea in [you] *Gotta Serve Somebody*:

> You might be a rock 'n' roll addict prancing on the stage
> You might have drugs at your command, women in a cage
> You may be a businessman or some high-degree thief
> They may call you Doctor or they may call you Chief.
> But you're gonna have to serve somebody, yes indeed
> You're gonna have to serve somebody
> Well, it may be the devil or it may be the Lord
> But you're gonna have to serve somebody.

This is an idea that lies at the heart of Jesus' teaching. In Luke 22 he will say, "The kings of the Gentiles lord it over them; and those in authority over them are called benefactors. But not so with you; rather the greatest among you must become like the youngest, and the leader like one who serves."

And Paul in Philippians 2 will ask us to be like Jesus: "Do nothing from selfish ambition or conceit, but in humility regard others as better than yourselves. Let each of you look not to your own interests, but to the interests of others. Let the same mind be in you that was in Christ Jesus, who, though he was in the form of God, did not regard equality with God as something to be exploited, but emptied himself, taking the form of a slave."

The answer Jesus gives to the disciples, an invitation to serve, still begs the question: How is this consolation for a defeated spirit? This is a critical question. I played Roberta Flack's version of *Come, Ye Disconsolate* through the church's sound system once, following a sermon, and it was too much for some of the congregation to bear. Here bring your wounded hearts, she sang. Here bring your anguish.

Theologian Dorothee Sölle speaks of the disconsolate, mute suffering of those who live abandoned in the world by the world. The Psalms, she argues, or writing like Lamentations give a voice to unbearable silence. The song sung by Roberta Flack becomes part of this company of articulated pain. Spoken, sung, the source of the pain becomes conscious and part of the shared consciousness of a people. The trajectory of this process of articulation leads to a new identity that is empowered by becoming fundamentally social, and leads to a society that is empowered to act.

Jesus calls us to the cross. The call to the way of the cross is no call to resign ourselves, without power, to the way things are. The call to the way of the cross is, more creatively, a call to live the life of Christ, as servants, in company with all the broken and bruised and crucified in every forgotten corner of our world. This is our consolation. With this company we build a new world. The service we are called to is no mere obedience to an existing relationship in which we find ourselves powerless. This is service as solidarity with those who suffer, and it can change the world.

The consolation that God will fix it without our human participation is the rather popular but really rather infantile distortion of the more rigorous good news that inevitably involves our discipleship, and therefore our own inner transformation, our own liberation, our own resurrection.

In solidarity with Christ, we are invited to take up the way of the cross. This is salvation in the blood of Christ poured out for many, which is also, inescapably, in our discipleship, our own blood poured out for many. We learn to cry together with the voices of lamentation. We learn to be silent together with those whose suffering has robbed them of song. "Come to the feast of love," Roberta Flack sings. "Come, ever knowing / Earth has no sorrow but heaven can remove."

Proper 23 C: "Join in with God's laughter"

Luke 17:11–19

The original version of Psalm 100 that we call "Old 100", attributed to the Scottish clergyman William Kethe, said to be written when he was in exile in Geneva, has "Him serve with fear, his praise forth tell" in the third line.

The version of Kethe's translation that made it into the Scottish Metrical Psalms has "Him serve with mirth, his praise forth tell."

Though to be fair the word "fear" here means something more like 'respect', the difference between fear and mirth nevertheless defines something important about the Jesus movement, and informs what is going on in Luke 17 when the healed leper turns back to give thanks. What happens around Jesus is much more like mirth than fear.

Richard Dawkins says anybody who is good only for being afraid of God is not really being good at all. Inducing fear, he says, is religion's thing. Perhaps the Bible says "Do not be afraid" as often as it does because there is much to fear.

If Dawkins is correct, then the world of Jesus was a world full of fear. The people who followed Jesus lived in a world swarming with religions of all sorts and riddled with religious sects anxious to find favor with God. They were surrounded by temples and shrines and priests and oracles, mysteries and sacred rituals of all sorts. This was what the Hellenistic world was like. It was a nervous age, when the population worshipped like an anxious gambler covering the table with bets. Not everyone was a Jew, and Judaism itself could be affected by all this.

Notice the dynamics of our story. Surely Jesus would have agreed with the prophet Micah that the Lord desires doing justice, loving mercy and walking humbly with God, and not sacrifice. But he sends the company of lepers to make their claim on the Temple anyway, and the story seems to assume that dutifully following the elaborate provisions of the Law will bring healing. This isn't like the story Luke borrowed from Mark (see Luke 5:12–14), where Jesus heals a leper, then sends him on to the Temple to have his cleansing verified. Jesus doesn't heal the ten lepers.

Instead, they experience healing along the way. And Jesus comments (Luke 17:19) that it is their faith that has made them well. The point seems to be similar to a commonplace among seventeenth century Calvinists like John Abernethy, who said, in *A Christian and Heavenly Treatise*, "Desire for grace in the want of grace is grace itself." God is already present in the desire for God. Healing is there in the desire for healing.

What is happening here is what is happening throughout Luke's narrative. The marginalized who desire healing, reconciliation, forgiveness, become the insiders. From Mary in the opening scenes of the Gospel, who rejoices that God has "looked with favor on the lowliness of his servant," to the thief on the cross who asks Jesus to remember him when he comes into his kingdom, the longing heart becomes the place where the Spirit can be found. This is the pattern that gives the overall shape of the Gospel of Luke, a Gospel filled with mirth. You don't get people threatened with being thrown into the outer darkness to weep and gnash their teeth here, as in some other Gospels.

The pattern is reinforced by the information that the one who returns to thank Jesus is a Samaritan, Judaism's pariah cousin. In Luke, the theater of God's action is among those who are capable of hunger and thirst, not among the richly robed of the Jerusalem Temple. I remember many years ago reading a brief piece in *The Expository Times* arguing that the center of Christendom is much more to be found on a Sunderland council estate than it is in Westminster Abbey. This is the kind of argument Luke is making.

Jesus nevertheless sends the lepers to be healed in Jerusalem because it is at the traditional center that the claim must first be made. The healing of the ten lepers takes place along the way as Jesus journeys to Jerusalem, remember. "Jerusalem, Jerusalem," he will cry on his arrival there. "The city that kills the prophets and stones those who are sent to it!" I think of what Paul VI said in *Evangelii Nuntiandi*: "The Church stands ever in need of evangelization."

But evangelized by whom? asks Leonardo Boff in his book *New Evangelization: Good News to the Poor*. By the poor, in the first place, in their hunger for justice, their desire for solidarity and their demand for participation in determining their destiny. By contemporary culture, with its spirit of critical analysis and dialogue, its tolerance of and engagement with otherness, its wealth of resources in scientific enquiry and the human sciences. And the Roman Catholic Church, Boff says, needs to be evangelized by the rest of the Christian churches in ecumenical engagement, and by other religions. This goes for the United Reformed Church, as well, of course. We need to live on the margins of our institutional life with mirth, not fear.

Can we be the Church where this happens? Try singing Kate Compston's song, *I dream of a church that joins in with God's laughter*, to the tune The Bard of Armagh:

> I dream of a church that joins in with God's loving
> as she bends to embrace the unlovely and lost,
> a church that can free, by its sharing and daring,
> the imprisoned and poor, and then shoulder the cost.

Proper 24 C: "Stone and flesh"

Jeremiah 31:27–34; Luke 18:1–8

Jeremiah looks forward to a time when that original, animating word of God will be written not in tablets of stone but in the passionate flesh of the human heart, a time when the word of God will not be a command from the past to be obeyed but a matter of the heart's desire.

The past often carries our deepest loyalties. The Archbishop of Canterbury celebrated the completion of the reconstruction and restoring of St Teilo's church at the Welsh National Folk Museum. Originally built in the High Middle Ages not far from Swansea and then regularly modified, St Teilo's was painstakingly dismantled stone-by-stone and reconstructed over a period of twenty years. I've been aware of this huge project and have watched its progress with great anticipation since I first arrived in Cardiff in 1988.

When it was first built in the thirteenth century, St Teilo's was a fresh local example of an exciting international style of ecclesiastical architecture in a European church that was itself progressive and theologically innovative. And since they hadn't invented the idea of Listed Buildings in those days, St Teilo's was regularly modified according to need and the evolving styles of the day. We sometimes forget that the Middle Ages was in its own time a contemporary, living, progressive culture.

Today, St Teilo's is a museum piece, no longer adaptable to the changing realities of a living community. We can agree with Rowan Williams that it is an exciting building to be in. The vibrancy of its colorful wall paintings testifies to a liveliness in medieval Christianity that was lost in the Victorian Gothic Revival's preference for walls of bare grey stone. The Victorian imagination caricatured medieval piety as otherworldly and mysterious and best remembered in churches that looked like the ruined choirs of places like Tintern Abbey. St Teilo's is indeed an exciting building to be in. But at the end of the day St Teilo's position in St Fagan's is to remind us of what used to be, but is no more.

Is this a good thing, or is this a bad thing? Jeremiah seems to imply that it is a good thing to put the stone relics of the past where they belong, however venerated, in the museums, and get on with a living faith. Matthew Arnold, for instance, at the very time in the mid-nineteenth century that the Anglican Church was attempting to recapture a medieval past, wrote in the poem "Dover Beach" of faith as a withdrawing tide, and of the sound of the sea of faith's melancholy, long, withdrawing roar, retreating down the naked shingles of the world.

While the heritage people rebuild what used to be, honest eyes, says Arnold, look at the world and see "neither joy, nor love, nor light, / Nor certitude, nor peace, nor help for pain" in a world "where ignorant armies clash by night."

In the face of such a dark and meaningless world, Arnold takes a defiant stand: "Ah, love," he says, "let us be true / To one another!" I will never forget the impact this defiant stance against a meaningless world had for me in the days after John Fitzgerald Kennedy was assassinated. "Ah, love, let us be true to one another!"

It seems to me Jeremiah is saying something very similar. The stone props of a faith lived by mere obedience to the past are like museum artifacts, things of the past. A childlike obedience to authority has never been enough to sustain the Church. We need an adult faith. What counts is understanding God's agenda and ownership of that agenda in the way we hope and a sense of responsibility for the future that takes action; what counts is our own *desire* for new possibilities; what counts is being true to one another in ways that bring the love of Christ to a harsh and empty world.

This poor widow in Luke 18, for instance, is less a model for the persistence of our intercessory prayers than she is a model for the belief that the world doesn't have to stay the same, that the world can change, that justice is possible. You remember the story. She comes again and again to the judge appealing for justice against those who oppress her. The judge isn't interested in justice, but he grants her request simply that he might be left in peace.

This judge embodies everything Matthew Arnold says about the emptiness and meaninglessness of a world in which there is "neither joy nor love, nor light, / Nor certitude, nor peace, nor help for pain." The judge fears neither God nor neighbor. And yet he gives in, because the woman never gives up.

God is in this woman as Jesus tells his disciples that God will be in them as God is in Jesus. The word of God lives written in her heart as a hunger and thirst for righteousness, and she will not be put off. She prays as we do, that God's will might be done here on earth, just as it is in heaven.

She's not very nice, is she? She's actually a bit like what we call 'bolshie'. She isn't interested in resignation to what life throws at her. Her faith is no childlike acceptance, nor is it an unquestioning obedience to creeds carved in stone. Her faith is a passionate commitment to new possibilities. Her faith is the substance of things hoped for. Her faith is the stubborn refusal to accept the world as it is. And Jesus asks, when the Son of Man comes, will he find such faith anywhere?

I don't think this story is about offering assurance that persistent intercessory prayers will be answered, so much as it is an assurance that such persistence is the basic stance of the Christian faith in general.

Without that persistent, burning desire in our own hearts that puts flesh on God's desires and rattles the cages of the authorities, we can be assured that nothing will happen, and we can be assured that the church, without such burning desire in the heart of a living community, will never be anything more for us than a cold, stone artifact of the past.

Proper 25 C: "Call for reformation"

Luke 18:9–14

Luke 18 tells a tale of hypocrisy. Two men are absorbed in prayer, the one an upright Pharisee, the other a spiritually marooned tax collector. Do you know what it feels like to be spiritually marooned? Something about the world you live in or the shape your life's got into has cast you off on a deserted, arid landscape from which there seems to be no escape.

The Pharisee, as well he might, thanks God that he is not like this tax collector. In his prayer, he lists all his own righteous qualities. He fasts twice a week. He tithes ten percent of his income. But he doesn't include in this list a spirit of compassion for the spiritually down-and-out. It is easy for us to label this Pharisee as a hypocrite.

My favorite story about hypocrisy is the movie *Paper Moon*, starring Ryan and Tatum O'Neal. Ryan O'Neal plays a character who runs a criminally hypocritical Bible-selling scam, pretending to be an agent of the Kansas Bible Company. He finds vulnerable recently-widowed women by reading the obituaries in local papers, calls on them, and pretends to be delivering collect-on-delivery Bibles their recently deceased husbands had ordered. He preys on their emotions with his sleazy sanctimonious sympathy while charging them extortionist prices for the Bibles their guilt and remorse compel them to pay for.

A friend of my older brother used to be a door-to-door Bible salesman. He would entertain people at parties with the emotionally entrapping sales pitch he would put into play should anyone be so unlucky to answer the doorbell when he called. You can imagine.

But sleazy, duplicitous scams like this aren't really what hypocrisy is all about. The true hypocrite, French author André Gide once said, ceases to perceive deception. The true hypocrite is the one who lies with sincerity. And the point Jesus seems to be making over and over again is that such self-deceiving hypocrisy seems so sadly to be the prevailing character of religious community. People seem to flock to temples in order to be deceived by fictions they find more palatable than the truth, and no one seems to believe these fictions more fervently than those who proclaim them. Organized religion seems to become organized hypocrisy by its very nature.

Martin Luther, for instance, sparked the reformation of the Church by protesting against the selling of indulgences in the same way one might protest against the door-to-door Bible salesman's emotional manipulation of vulnerable widows. Only those who were selling indulgences were by and large sincere, even when the pieces of paper they sold people to guarantee remission of sins were being sold to fund the lavish gold and marble construction of St. Peter's in Rome, even when their success was clearly a symptom of people's fears and deep insecurities. Luther never doubted their sincerity. He tried to open the Church's eyes to something insidiously wrong about its best intentions. In its belief that it could mediate the love of God for the disconsolate in this way, the Church would up preying upon their vulnerability and lost the sense of the grace it had been entrusted to proclaim.

The Church has a way of turning in upon itself in this way. You see it today in the way the Church's growth or even survival becomes her key objective, while the surface message remains one of welcome and hospitality, manipulating the emotional needs of today's spiritually marooned. It begins to look, at the worst, like pyramid marketing schemes, or, at best, like the evangelical marketing strategies of Amway. In *Amway: The Cult of Free Enterprise,* Stephen Butterfield describes how Amway "sells a marketing and motivational system, a cause, a way of life, in a fervid emotional atmosphere of rallies and political religious revivalism." In their pursuit of success churches can get like this. The Church in its pursuit of consumers becomes a hollow shell of pious practice and emotional enthusiasm that has lost all connection with the selfless love it is called to mediate to a broken world. It becomes like the Pharisee, hollow. Far from liberating its members, it cripples them.

Why does this happen? Terry Pratchett, in *Small Gods*, tells of a novice who asks where religion comes from. Here is the answer he gets: "There forms around God a cell of praise and ceremonies and buildings and priests and authority until at last God dies." Religion itself smothers God, the novice learns, as it comes to be. And the tragedy, Pratchett goes on to say, is that no one seems to notice.

That is the kind of deep-seated hypocrisy Jesus condemns here, and that is why Jesus is set against the religious establishment, or, as Dietrich Bonhoeffer would say, set against religion itself. Bonhoeffer's call for a religionless Christianity comes right out of the heart of this parable of the Pharisee and the tax collector. We still haven't found a way out of the problem it sets.

Proper 26 C: "The Heretical Imperative"

Isaiah 1:10–18; Psalm 32:1–7; Luke 19:1–10

Religion has a way of getting in the way of our spiritual journey. It becomes its own stumbling block. That's the sense of the crowd gathered to welcome Jesus into Jericho, full of enthusiasm, but blocking access to the one person in the city who really needs to see him: Zacchaeus, short Zacchaeus, who is reduced to having to climb a sycamore tree to see what everybody else is seeing.

The scene reminds me of a story I was told early on when I arrived here in the UK, how Jamaicans arriving here in the 1950s and 1960s tried to get into our churches, but were turned away, often invited to try the more lively church down the street, when such a church was available. To be fair, such rejection may not have been simple racism. The stiff, itchy-wool formality of British Christianity in those days was not just a matter of culture, but faith. The churches simply couldn't comprehend how they might accommodate the newly-arrived Jamaicans. Well, maybe it was racism. In any case, it led to the establishment of separate, black-led churches, strong in today's London, while the institutions that had turned them away atrophy.

You get the same story in our Old Testament reading for this morning. Isaiah addresses Judah as Sodom and Gomorrah, but the sin he rails against is neither sexual immorality nor inhospitality but excess religion:

> "What to me is the multitude of your sacrifices?" says the Lord; "I have had enough of burnt offerings... Learn to do good; seek justice, rescue the oppressed, defend the orphan, plead for the widow."

Again, it is religion that is getting in the way.

The Gospel of Luke from start to finish is about celebrating the inclusion of society's outsiders, from the shepherds who hurry down to Bethlehem to see the newborn baby to the disconsolate disciples on the road to Emmaus, their hopes dashed by what those at the center of the religious and political establishment have done to the Jesus movement, who finally recognize Jesus still present and undefeated in their midst through the simple act of breaking bread among strangers.

In the Gospel of Luke it is never the big-hatted religiously proper people who see what Jesus is all about. It is always the odd ones, the misfits and the excluded, people like Zacchaeus who are surviving in a hostile colonial economy by collecting taxes for Caesar. It's the woman who survives by working the streets, or the blind man reduced to begging. These are the ones who can see. There is something about the pain of exclusion and the struggle for basic survival that opens people to what Jesus is all about.

The guardians of traditional religion not only never get the point. There is something about their agenda that actually works in a contrary direction to the redemptive, compassionate, gracious ways of God.

These who experience exclusion, on the contrary, become the prophetic voices that tell us what the church is like. They understand from their own bitter experience how cold and uncaring a church can be that pursues a self-absorbed religious agenda, its festivals and carol services, its liturgical splendor, its emotional song-singing, the precision of its obedient biblical literalism, its anxiety over its own personal and institutional security, and its consequent blindness to justice in the world around it.

Religious crowds seem by their very nature to become in-groups, with arcane, coded ways of doing things. I remember when I first came to Wales almost twenty years ago now someone suggested we sing "*Bread of Heaven*" for one particular service. I couldn't find *Bread of Heaven* anywhere in the index, and then I finally discovered she was talking about *Guide Me, O Thou Great*

Jehovah.

William Williams wrote *Guide Me, O Thou Great Jehovah,* or *Bread of Heaven,* as we call it, in 1745. *Bread of Heaven* tells the same basic story of the redemption of the discarded told in the story of Zacchaeus. In *Bread of Heaven* it is the Exodus story, where God, in effect, says to Hebrew slaves in Egypt, I'm coming to your house for tea tonight.

On Bardsey Island there is a tombstone of a farmer who died in 1883 that says his favorite hymn was *Pen Calfaria.* What hymn was that? Can you imagine? Of course, it was the original Welsh version of *Guide Me, O Thou Great Jehovah,* known by the tag of another verse, *Pen Calfaria,* or *Hill of Calvary.* The new community we celebrate in the story of Zacchaeus is the community of shared suffering we know from the cross, from the three crosses on Calvary's hill, the new, authentic community we find outside the city, among the condemned, on the place they called The Place of the Skull.

Jesus offers us what the sociologist Peter Berger calls the heretical imperative, the necessity, really, of choosing a place to stand in God's company that is often outside the gates of the religious establishment, as *Pen Calfaria* is always outside the gates of the religious establishment.

Somehow, in order to maintain our integrity as a Christian people, we need to find a way of living self-critically in this way, so that what we do – the hymns we sing, the festivals we celebrate – all this becomes a means of liberation and affirmation of those who look in from the outside, hungering for a word of grace, but can't get in. How can we do that? How can we practice, as a religious community, what Dietrich Bonhoeffer called a religionless Christianity?

I remember a Catholic sister who was a member of the chaplaincy team at Birmingham University telling me that the bread we break at communion doesn't really become the body of Christ until it is broken and shared with people who suffer from real physical hunger outside the walls of the church. The hunger of our own hearts ought to tell us that the journey taken by those who sing *Bread of Heaven* toward that deeper and richer integrity of life lived with God is a journey that necessarily takes us outside the gates to sit at table with unlikely neighbors.

Proper 27 C: "Remembering forward"

Luke 21:5–19

I remember the mathematics teacher we had when I was 14 years old telling us about marching through Paris in a parade celebrating the armistice at the end of the Great War. He told us of all the girls who threw themselves on the soldiers as they marched by, slobbering all over them, he said, as he grinned and made this gesture of wiping the slobber off his cheeks.

They say peace is something infinitely more than the mere cessation of hostilities. But for those who experienced the senseless mechanized butchery of that war and the laying down of arms that finally came in 1918, the end of hostilities was enough, at least if you were on the victorious side. The storm was over. The rainbow hung in the sky. The dove had returned to the ship carrying the twig that was evidence of new life. Sometimes the end of hostilities is enough.

Ever since that Armistice Day we have struggled to commemorate the peace by recalling the lives that had been lost to war. The intention was to create the social will to remember, as the Dalai Lama said shortly after 9/11, how totally inappropriate war and all forms of violence are in settling disputes.

Remembrance Day needs to stand with other days like International Peace Day or Hiroshima Day that perhaps more clearly look forward to a Peace on Earth that is something more than a poetic dream. But early on the government feared a focus on peace would lead to anti-war and anti-government protests. Lord Curzon, President of the Armistice Day Committee in 1921, even argued that 11 November should not be "a day of mourning" but instead should become "the commemoration of a great day in the country's history." The cenotaph tradition, with the Last Post and the singing of *I Vow to Thee My Country*, has maintained a military focus, though the day is not without an underlying controversy, even with its overwhelming endorsement by the media and the government bureaucrats. Politicians and news presenters start wearing red poppies in October, and even the free churches feel the pressure to celebrate Remembrance Sunday as well as Remembrance Day. Those who wear the white poppy of peace are met with scorn, as if hope for peace dishonors the dead.

Fred Kaan, who spent his teenage years in occupied Holland and refused to join the Hitler Youth, wrote, in a Remembrance Day hymn, "how hate and war diminish humankind," and calls us to "remember forward to a world restored."

How do we remember forward? How can we step out of the bitter memory of the past to imagine, together, the engagements with others that make for peace? I remember the year in Chicago when I chaired our Interfaith Clergy-Rabbi Association, and I arranged for an interfaith commemoration of Yom Hashoah, Holocaust Memorial Day.

In the coffee time after the service a woman came up to me, a woman glowing with visible enthusiasm, to tell me that she was a member of the Holocaust Survivors Association and to ask me if one of their members could come to speak at our church. This was an astonishing experience. It was as if she was filled with evangelical fervor, filled with a message so overflowing with joy that it had to be shared. How could her experience of the death camps, of the soul and body destroying slave labor, of the determination to destroy her people as if they were vermin, how could all this become a message of such joy? How could bad news become good news, evangel?

Precisely, I thought, because her story needed to become our story. Kept to itself in the community of those who suffered, it only descends into bitterness and rancor. Shared, it breaks down walls of separation and becomes cause for hoping together for a different way of being the world together.

Only when we have built bridges connecting communities

that enable those communities to share one another's memories and dreams, only then will we have real hope for peace. Kenneth Bigley, for instance, was a civil engineer kidnapped in Baghdad in 2004 and executed. We were told on the late afternoon news that his memorial service included readings from the Koran, a detail that was curiously dropped from later transmissions of the story. Though it was a detail the public may not have wished to hear, it is just such a bridge-building witness that can confront the violent agendas of this century. No other memorial could better redeem Ken Bigley's death and liberate it from the grip of enmity that holds our world so fast today. But this isn't what the public wants to know.

The church historian Martin Marty, early on in the Iraq war, reported that as he travelled from church to church across my home country listening to prayers commemorating the deaths of American soldiers, he began to wonder what had happened to Christianity, the faith of Jesus whose cross was supposed to have broken down the dividing walls of enmity to create new communities. Why were we only praying for our own?

The British medical journal *The Lancet,* for instance, has estimated that some 601,000 Iraqis died of violence through the end of 2006. In Fallujah alone there were 1,600 Iraqi deaths. The number of American deaths in Iraq, including non-hostile deaths, stood at 4,405 up to May 2012. The journalist John Pilger has shown how *The Lancet* report has been systematically suppressed by the majority of British news media. Propaganda only gives us what we want to hear.

But it is not just that the numbers of Iraqi dead were missing from our public consciousness. There was also the active hostility, as in the notorious physical, psychological, and sexual abuse, including torture of prisoners at Abu Ghraib, exposed in 2004. Also in 2004, the *Independent* reported that the Iraqi interim government had begun restoring the monument to Iraq's eight year American-supported war with Iran, a monument that had been desecrated by American soldiers who painted crude versions of American military insignia and slogans over the Iraqi cenotaph's 600,000 names.

It may be that Iraq's war of aggression against the new Islamic Republic of Iran was only the misguided, grandiose folly of a mad man. But we could use virtually the same language to describe the madness of the First World War, a war sparked by an isolated incident of violence that then erupted in unstoppable ethnic hatred, a war fuelled by European steel and armaments industries and driven by the shabby rhetoric of patriotism, the piety of Christian soldiering and an upper class dream of honor that drove millions upon millions of young men to an absurd death. And Britain was like touch paper waiting to be ignited in 1914. Cecil Eby, in *The Road to Armageddon: The Martial Spirit in English Popular Literature,* shows that by 1889 there were forty thousand brass bands in Britain, playing more military marches than anything else. London alone had five hundred music halls noted for the singing of patriotic choruses. In the forty years preceding the Great War over sixty books of fiction were published on the theme of foreign invasions, mostly from Germany. The denominations, especially the Church of England, joined in the war drumming. Triumphal music like *Onward, Christian Soldiers,* composed by Arthur Sullivan, was typical fare for the latter years of nineteenth century Britain. We need to do it differently. We need to remember forward to a time when there may be no more war.

World War I was believed to be the "war to end all wars" in the sense that it was thought to be the final Armageddon battle against the Antichrist. In our Gospel lesson for this morning people come to Jesus to ask him if the horrors they are experiencing are signs of the day of divine judgment. He says no. He adds that there will be many voices rallying public emotion claiming to speak in the name of God, claiming to speak with Messianic authority, calling down the fire of heaven. But these voices are not the voice of God. Those who come to question Jesus are anxious. They see their world falling apart. Jesus tells us to be patient.

The Gospel of Luke was of course written after the fall of Jerusalem. So what is made to seem like prophecy here is actually remembering. Luke's readers see their world fallen apart and judged in some final way. But Luke's Jesus says No, it has not been judged in some final way. Nor should we today see the violence we are witnessing as a sign of final irretrievable collapse. In effect, Jesus says what we are witnessing is an open-ended time calling for patience, a time when we can still remember forward to a time of reconciliation and build the kind of communities that make that reconciliation happen.

A group of witnesses gathered in London's Trafalgar Square to read out a list of some 5,000 Iraqi civilians who had died in the war by then, or, rather, the names of those whose names were known, for the actual total was far higher even then. Civilian casualties are a growing phenomenon of modern warfare. At the beginning of the last century only 15% of wartime casualties were civilians. By the middle of that century the percentage rose to about 50%. Today, despite all the propaganda about precision bombing, civilian casualties represent more than 90% of the total, and many of these are women and children. We see this particularly in Syria. Those who fall in battle today are predominately not soldiers who have made the final sacrifice, as we sing in the song, but civilians, mothers and their infants, elderly people with their wisdom, young people with dreams. They have not died for a cause or to protect our freedom. They have died because of the absurdity of war.

The astrophysicist Stephen Hawking was prominently among those reading out the list of names of the Iraqi civilian dead. Hawking apologized that the computer through which he speaks could not properly handle the Arabic names he was given to read. And so might we. Even those who have managed to pronounce Welsh find Arabic full of strange and awkward sounds. But knowing and reading out the names of the Iraqi dead is an important Christian witness. If we are ever going to be effective witnesses for the Peace on Earth of the Prince of Peace we must learn to name those who have died by the power of our weapons, no matter how emotionally difficult we find it to pronounce their names. We must be brave enough to rise above the public pressure of an easy, poppy-buying patriotism to remember them, and intentional enough about what we believe to let their stories and their cut-off dreams become our stories and our dreams. This is what it means to be Christian.

Proper 28 C: "The Sense of an Ending"

Isaiah 65:17–25; Luke 21:5–19

The disciples in Luke 21 are worried about what is going to happen in the soon-to-come divine judgment that comes in the 'End Times' scenario. The Church uses these dark November days of long nights slouching toward the winter solstice as a kind of metaphor for the Last Days. We always have readings like this at this time of year.

Some take the End Times quite literally, as that strange doomsday sect of Russian Orthodox people who holed up in a Russian cave when their spiritual leader, Pyotr Kuznetsov, told them that the world was ending soon and the only way for them to save themselves was to hide underground. Doomsday prophets pop up regularly around the world. A Korean group, the Mission for the Coming Days, said the end would come on 28 October 1992. John Hinkle, the minister of Christ Church in Los Angeles, said it would happen on 9 June 1994. Radio evangelist Harold Camping had May 21, 2011 and then revised it to October 21, 2011. Apocalypse enthusiasts widely believe the year 2012 is going to spell the end of things. It apparently says so in an ancient Mayan calendar.

Scientists also take the end of the world literally, but read different texts. They say our world will end 5 billion years from now when the sun dies out. The end might come in only 1.4 million years when a star that is hurtling towards us at 50,000 k/h smashes into our solar system. Or we might go out like the dinosaurs when a big piece of rock hits the planet, as happens about once every hundred years, the last one hitting remote Siberia just after 7 a.m. on 30 June 1908. Our world might end tomorrow.

The prophet Isaiah in our Old Testament reading says God creates a new heaven and a new earth when children take a central place in the life of God's people. When children no longer die in infancy, when children are no longer born for calamity but are blessed by the Lord to grow up and live their lives full of joy and productivity, the old world has come to an end in a community that has chosen to live in ways that honor the vulnerable among them. The end of the world is a matter of choice and discipleship.

In Luke 21 Jesus and his disciples are taking a tour of the magnificent marble and gold Jerusalem temple. In the back rooms of the temple, according to the Jewish historian Josephus, there hung a thousand ornate gold-embroidered vestments for the priests. This was religious life at its finest. The disciples, the simple village boys from the Galilee, stand there with mouths open in wonder. But according to Jesus, all this is coming down. This world is coming to an end. This isn't the kind of religious world we need.

The disciples panic, thinking this really is the end of the world. But Jesus says, "No." Lots of bogus leaders will come out from under the woodwork who will try to convince you that they are the messiah, that they have the final truth, that the end of the world is coming. Don't be deceived, Jesus cautions.

City United Reformed Church's Grade II listed building might be torn down. Nations might rise against nation and people against people. There might be earthquakes and floods and bird flu and Schmallenberg virus and the Euro might collapse. You might be tossed out of the synagogues and arrested and persecuted. You can actually count on all this happening. But it wouldn't be the end of the world, Jesus says.

The end of the world comes when, in the middle of all this, what you really believe and are committed to begins to come clear to you and, faced with a crisis of loyalties, you become aware that a world you once believed in no longer exists for you. It's like what the civil rights demonstrators used to say back in my young adult years in the States. When they stick the attack dogs on you, you know right away whose side you are on. A new heaven and a new earth have been born – something to believe in and a place to stand on what you believe.

When we talk about creating a new heaven and a new earth we mean just that, literally. A new heaven and a new earth will be a different world. It will include communities that do not despoil the earth, communities that do not drive the vulnerable into deeper poverty, communities that commit themselves to reconciliation and peacemaking in a violent, competitive world, that our children and a generation yet unborn might live.

Christ the King C: "We preach Christ crucified"

Jeremiah 23:1–6; Luke 23:32–43

A Dutchman was fumbling about for the correct way to address the Queen of the Netherlands. The Queen noticed his discomfort and mercifully cut in to say, "Oh, just call me Majesty."

It's the down-to-earth bicycle-riding nature of Dutch royalty that gives this story its particular appeal.

On Christ the King Sunday the one the Book of Revelation calls "King of kings" is shown crucified in the company of thieves. The kingly title seems to fit uncomfortably, like a royal joke. One of our Good Friday hymns calls him a "man discarded," a "clown of sorrows," a "scarecrow hoisted high," a "nonsense pointing nowhere." Surely there has never been so un-kingly a monarch in all of human history.

It is not only his un-kingly death that raises a problem. Early in the last century Albert Schweitzer described Jesus as an apocalyptic prophet, one of those visionaries proclaiming the soon-to-come end of the world. But the world did not, in fact, come to an end. There was no divine judgment. He was not, as the apocalyptic imagination would have it, crowned King of kings to lead a mighty army against the forces of unrighteousness. There was no Day of the Lord. So it isn't just the wretchedness of his un-kingly death that presents a problem. Jesus, according to Schweitzer, was a failed prophet, an apocalyptic prophet who made a mistake, a nonsense pointing nowhere, as the hymn says.

Perhaps we could speak of the crucified Jesus in the words Macbeth speaks on hearing of the death of his wife, Lady Macbeth:

> Life's but a walking shadow, a poor player
> That struts and frets his hour upon the stage

> And then is heard no more. It is a tale
> Told by an idiot, full of sound and fury,
> Signifying nothing.
> – Macbeth 5.5.24–28

The former Olympic champion Jonathan Edwards used to be a presenter on *Songs of Praise* before he gave up on Christianity. Reflecting on his years as an evangelical Christian athlete, he says "Believing in something beyond the self can have a hugely beneficial psychological impact, even if the belief is fallacious." Now Edwards has embraced the clear blue skies of a secular life that lacks, he says, any sense of purpose. At least he feels more honest these days, he says. As with Macbeth, time, for Edwards, just goes on, unfolding without purpose or meaning. There is no Day of the Lord. It is like it is in Luke 23, Jesus hanging on a cross, forsaken, keeping company with the world's condemned, a scarecrow hoisted high.

Put this scene firmly in your mind's eye. Jesus is hanging condemned in the company of thieves. This scene may not illustrate the diamond-crowned gold-brocade glory of kingship. But it does illustrate the grace of the kingdom of God, the vision that draws us together in fellowship with our most wretched neighbors. This little fellowship of three crosses illustrates a new kind of community that is different from Caesar's world. It is what we might call a counterworld to Caesar's world, unfathomable from the perspective of Caesar's world.

Was Jesus wrong? Was Jesus a failed prophet? Jesus will always be a failed prophet if we take his vision literally as have so many millenarian sects throughout history. Sometimes what passes for Christianity seeks to praise Jesus with the titles of Caesar. We haven't always got the point of what Christianity is all about. There are whole books of hymns and popular Christian songs glorifying the King of kings and Lord of lords with no reference to this counterworld kingdom of God central to what

Jesus preached and lived. It is common in what passes as Christianity for Christ to be celebrated as King with no reference to the kingdom he proclaimed. Where is the good news, if we take the kingdom out of the proclamation?

The message of the kingdom Jesus preached had deep roots. If we know our Bible we can see this good news of the kingdom of God deeply rooted in the Old Testament prophetic longing for a new world of justice and mercy when all the earth will be filled with the presence of God.

None of the extravagant visions of the prophets who laid the groundwork for the preaching of Jesus ever came true in a flat-footed, literal way. But they named the inequities of their day for what they were, they inspired confrontation, and they articulated hope for a new and more faithful way of being in the world nevertheless, as have the words of Jesus, as have the words of Peter and Paul and Luke and Matthew and Irenaeus and Chrysostom and Augustine and Anselm and Aquinas and Hildegard and Francis and Teresa and Luther and Martin Luther King and Oscar Romero and maybe even Rowan Williams, and certainly the minister of your local church. The grand prophetic word inspires us to live and act in hope, and act in hope that generations yet to come will also be filled with God's Word, and act. What we accomplish is provisional, partial, often short lived, but nevertheless real.

God help us if those hopes ever unfold in a final, totalizing sense. Then we get oppressive social/political structures like Caesar's Rome, or the kind of Calvinism that justified apartheid, or the Neo-Calvinism of the Christian Reconstructionist movement. When we Calvinists gain control of things, we begin to stink. There is something about Christianity that needs to remain provisional and poetic. Christianity always needs to be unfinished business, a matter of hope challenging the way things are.

St. David, the patron saint of Wales, said, "Do the small things that you have seen and heard in me" ('Gwnewch y pethau bychain a glywsoch ac a welsoch ynof fi'), a saying that defines poetry as well as discipleship. Sylvia Plath, for instance, once wrote,

> My poems do not turn out to be about Hiroshima, but about a child forming itself finger by finger in the dark. They are not about the terrors of mass extinction, but about the bleakness of the moon over a yew tree in a neighboring graveyard. Not about testaments of tortured Algerians, but about the night thoughts of a tired surgeon.

In Plath's images we see what rhetoric calls 'synecdoche', specific images that can represent something bigger and more general. It is in this poetic sense that the crucifixion of an obscure Galilean preacher outside the walls of a provincial city so many years ago gains such immense significance. The theologians of the Reformation used to say that the kingdom of God was hidden under its contrary, the cross. Those who cannot understand the connection between the cross and the brave new community Jesus was proclaiming are forever condemned to understanding Jesus as a failed prophet, and will never understand the meaning of resurrection.

We preach Christ crucified, a scandal to the Jews and folly to the Greeks, says Paul. An awful lot of Christians don't understand Christ crucified, either, and fumble about for the correct way to address their Savior. Should they address him as "Your Majesty"? They try all the titles derived from all the standard values of the world – kingship, power, authority, victory, the culture of domination and control, the whole baggage of patriarchal and hierarchical and imperialistic thinking that Jesus suffered so as a witness against. They just don't get the point.

We traditionally get our understanding of the authority of Jesus from a patriarchal and hierarchical world. But at the end of the day the only authority in Scripture is the authority of the servant, the authority of those who stand alongside the hungry as companions, and the authority of those who hunger themselves. Authority in the Bible, like majesty, comes from below. It is not the authority of a privileged text, but the authority of a liberating practice living beneath the text, a practice responding to the world's hunger. Authority in Scripture is found in the claims hunger makes on our hearts.

When we respond to claims like this, we glimpse the kingdom as a living, contemporary reality. All around us there are people who have been injured by a society that links dignity to special ability and grants an extraordinary hierarchy of rewards based on class. Communities are torn apart by private equity firms who take over industries, strip assets and discard employees. Following the collapse of mining, manufacturing and industrial jobs, a new working class of data entry clerks, shop assistants, care workers and food service workers barely scrapes by, with little or no union representation. And a service economy does insidious harm to the human soul. Modern management theory pits workers against one another as competitors, building insecurity into the system as a spur to greater productivity. And then there is the insecurity of migrant labor, and the loss of humanity among those who are trafficked.

When we listen to the stories of such people and allow those stories to change the way we think and act, they become an unlikely source of authority for us. When we obey them, we are obeying the authority of Jesus Christ crucified. Authority, for Christians, comes from below like this. When we obey it in what St. David called "the little things", in concrete acts of discipleship, however provisional, Jesus takes on flesh in us. Jesus comes to dwell among us as prophets foretold, and the kingdom of God is visible. So with longing hearts we call out in hope, "Come, Lord Jesus." We also celebrate: "Now is the day of salvation."